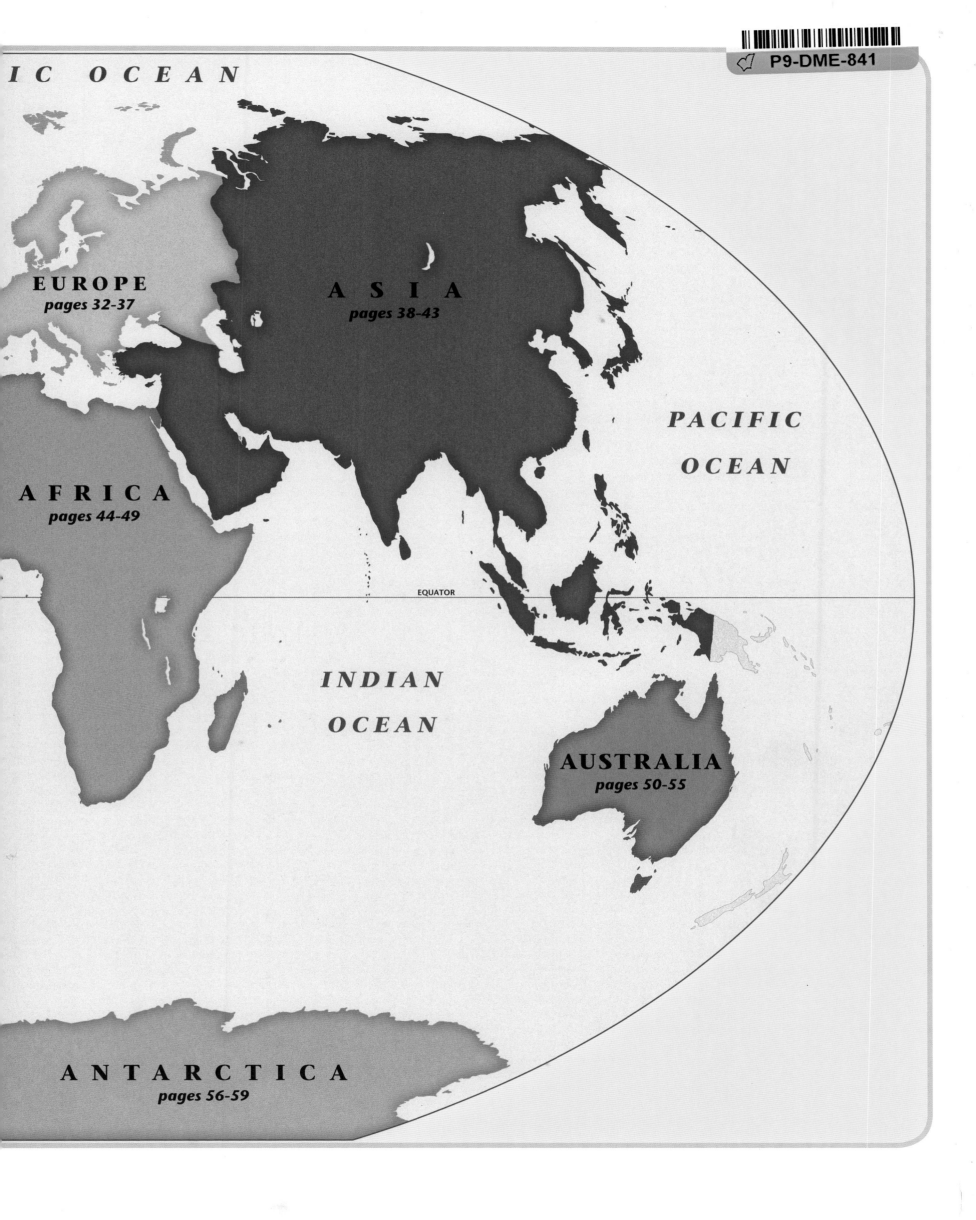

IC OCEAN

EUROPE
pages 32-37

A S I A
pages 38-43

AFRICA
pages 44-49

PACIFIC

OCEAN

EQUATOR

INDIAN

OCEAN

AUSTRALIA
pages 50-55

A N T A R C T I C A
pages 56-59

NATIONAL GEOGRAPHIC
KIDS™

BEGINNER'S
WORLD
ATLAS

**NATIONAL
GEOGRAPHIC**

Washington, D.C.

CONTENTS

To give you a sense of the wonderful diversity and rich traditions that make up our world, the children on this page and opposite are dressed in traditional outfits that represent their unique cultures. Look for them as they greet you on the opening pages of each continent.

WHAT IS A MAP?

A map is a drawing of a place as it looks from above. It is flat, and it is smaller than the place it shows. A map can help you find where you are and where you want to go.

MAPPING YOUR BACKYARD...

...FROM THE GROUND

From your backyard you see everything in front of you straight on. You have to look up to see your roof and the tops of trees. You can't see what's in front of your house.

...FROM HIGHER UP

From higher up you look down on things. You can see the tops of trees and things in your yard and in the yards of other houses in your neighborhood.

FINDING PLACES ON THE MAP

A **map** can help you get where you want to go. A map tells you how to read it by showing you a compass, a key, and a scale.

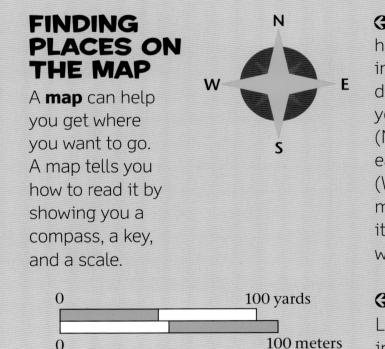

↩ A **compass** helps you travel in the right direction. It tells you where north (N), south (S), east (E), and west (W) are on your map. Sometimes it only shows where north is.

■	House
□	Store
□	School
□	Library
□	Play area
□	Water

↩ A **map key** helps you understand the symbols used by the mapmaker to show things like houses, play areas, and schools on the map.

↩ A **scale** tells you about distance on a map. Look at the scale on the map at the right. One inch is the same as traveling a hundred yards.

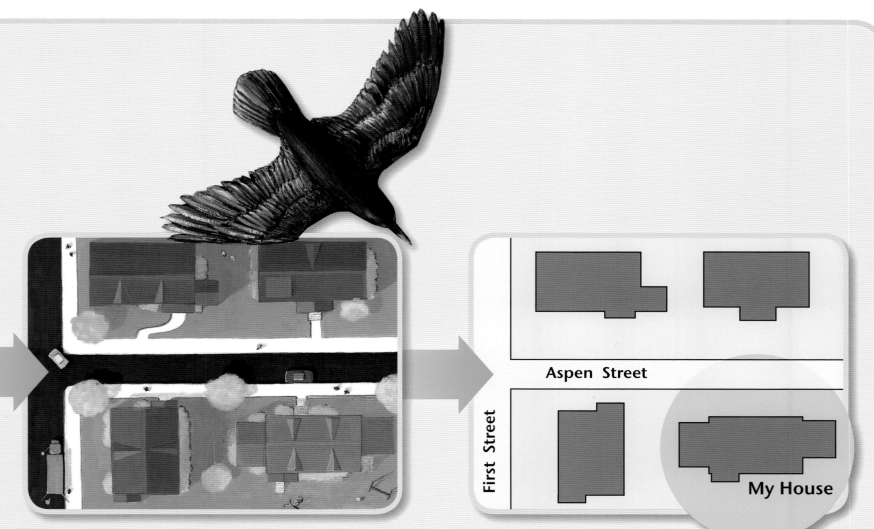

...FROM A BIRD'S-EYE VIEW

If you were a bird flying directly overhead, you would see only the tops of things. You wouldn't see walls, tree trunks, tires, or feet.

...ON A MAP

A map looks at places from a bird's-eye view. But it uses drawings called symbols to show things that don't move, such as houses.

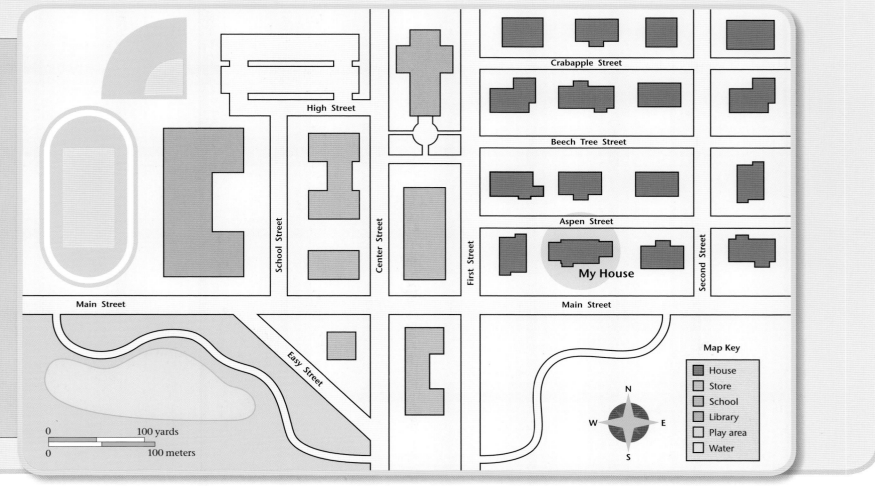

MAKING THE ROUND EARTH FLAT

From your backyard Earth probably looks flat. If you could travel into space like an astronaut, you would see that Earth is a giant ball with blue oceans, greenish brown land, and white clouds. Even in space you can only see the part of Earth facing you. To see the whole Earth at one time, you need a map. Maps take the round Earth and make it flat, so you can see all of it at one time.

NORTH AMERICA

EQUATOR

⟳ EARTH IN SPACE

From space you can see that Earth is round with oceans, land, and clouds. But you can see only half of Earth at one time.

SOUTH
AMERICA

☉ EARTH ON PAPER

If you could peel a globe like an orange, you could make Earth flat, but there would be spaces between the pieces. Mapmakers stretch the land and the water at the top and bottom to fill in the spaces. This is how a **map** lets you see the whole world all at once.

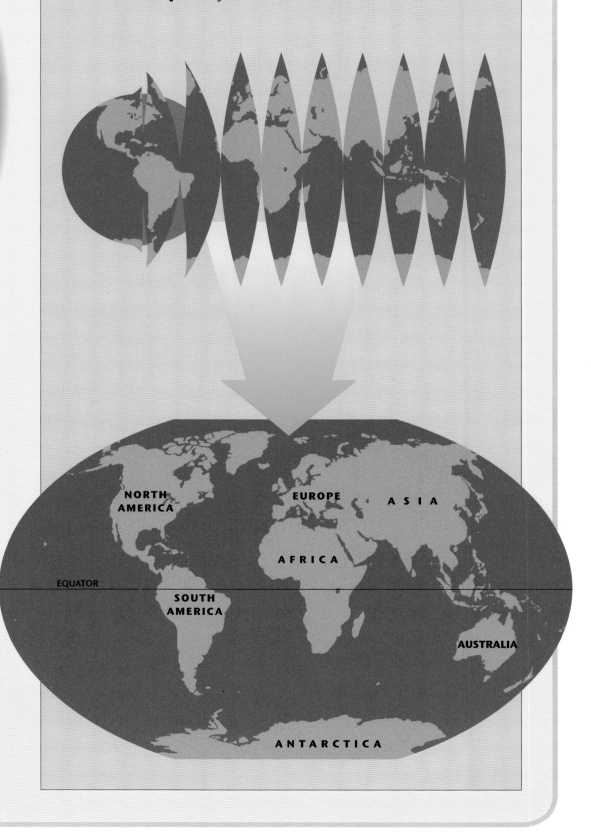

NORTH
AMERICA

EUROPE

ASIA

AFRICA

EQUATOR

SOUTH
AMERICA

AUSTRALIA

ANTARCTICA

☉ EARTH AS A GLOBE

A **globe** is a tiny model of Earth that you can put on a stand or hold in your hand. You have to turn it to see the other side. You still can't see the whole Earth at one time.

The **Equator** is an imaginary line around Earth's middle. Mapmakers show it as a solid or a dashed line on globes and maps.

WHAT THIS ATLAS WILL TEACH YOU

You hold the world in your hands as you look through the pages of this atlas. You will find a physical and a political map of each continent. Here is what you will learn about each one.

Mountains, Asia

Eiffel Tower, France

THE PHYSICAL WORLD

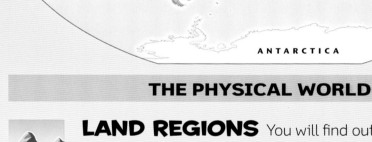

LAND REGIONS You will find out what kinds of land cover a continent. Does it have mountains and deserts? If so, where are they?

WATER You will learn about a continent's chief lakes, rivers, and waterfalls. You'll see that some continents have more water than others.

CLIMATE Climate is the weather of a place over many years. Some continents are colder and wetter or hotter and drier than others.

PLANTS You'll discover what kinds of plants grow on a particular continent.

Desert, North America

ANIMALS Continents each have certain kinds of animals. Did you know that tigers live in the wild only in Asia?

Camel, India

Grapes, Mediterranean region

Vancouver, Canada

Map of the political world showing continents, countries, and oceans including ARCTIC OCEAN, GREENLAND (Denmark), NORWAY, ICELAND, FINLAND, RUSSIA, CANADA, UNITED KINGDOM, UKRAINE, KAZAKHSTAN, MONGOLIA, FRANCE, SPAIN, TURKEY, SYRIA, IRAN, CHINA, JAPAN, UNITED STATES, MOROCCO, ALGERIA, LIBYA, EGYPT, SAUDI ARABIA, INDIA, PACIFIC OCEAN, MEXICO, CUBA, MAURITANIA, MALI, NIGER, CHAD, SUDAN, ETHIOPIA, THAILAND, VIETNAM, PHILIPPINES, NICARAGUA, VENEZUELA, GUYANA, SURINAME, LIBERIA, NIGERIA, DEMOCRATIC REPUBLIC OF THE CONGO, SOMALIA, COLOMBIA, ECUADOR, BRAZIL, ANGOLA, TANZANIA, ZAMBIA, EQUATOR, INDONESIA, PAPUA NEW GUINEA, PERU, BOLIVIA, PARAGUAY, NAMIBIA, MADAGASCAR, ATLANTIC OCEAN, PACIFIC OCEAN, CHILE, URUGUAY, ARGENTINA, SOUTH AFRICA, INDIAN OCEAN, AUSTRALIA, NEW ZEALAND, ANTARCTICA

Eurostar train, Europe

Coral reef, Pacific Ocean

THE POLITICAL WORLD

 COUNTRIES You will learn about the countries that make up a continent. Maps show country names in type like this: **UNITED STATES**

 **CITIES** You will find out which cities are the most important on a continent. The map key will tell you which cities are country capitals.

 PEOPLE You will learn where groups of people on a continent come from, where they live, what they do, how they have fun, and more.

LANGUAGES Many languages are spoken on most continents. Here you will find out which languages most people speak.

PRODUCTS This section will tell you which goods produced on a continent are most important to the people living there.

Schoolgirls, Vietnam

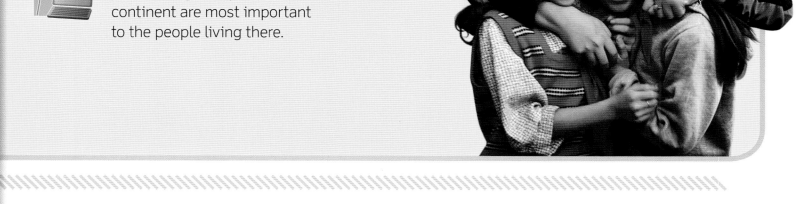

THE PHYSICAL WORLD

A physical map uses symbols to show where mountains, deserts, forests, and other features of the land are.

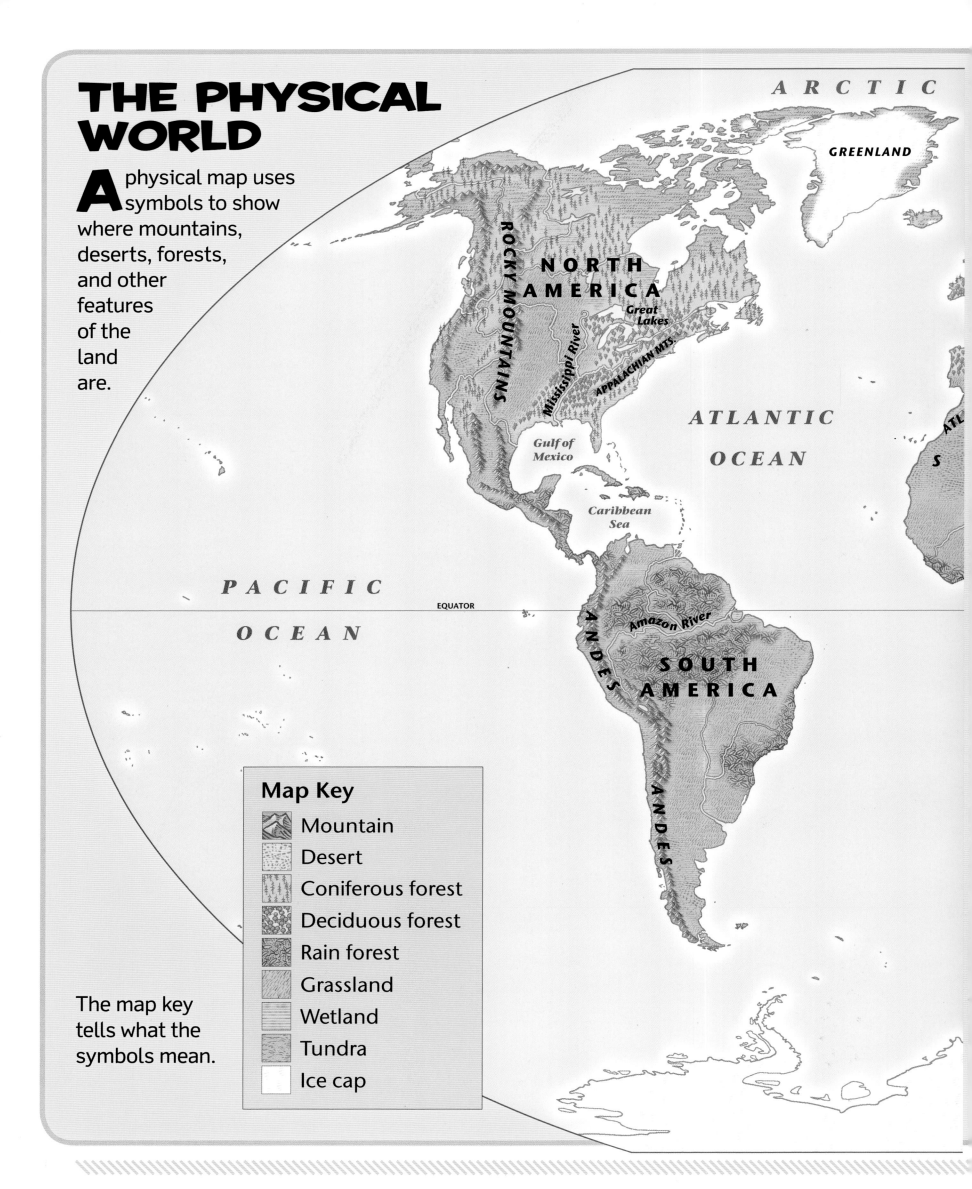

ARCTIC

GREENLAND

NORTH AMERICA

ROCKY MOUNTAINS

Great Lakes

Mississippi River

APPALACHIAN MTS.

Gulf of Mexico

ATLANTIC OCEAN

ATL

S

Caribbean Sea

PACIFIC

OCEAN

EQUATOR

Amazon River

ANDES

SOUTH AMERICA

ANDES

The map key tells what the symbols mean.

Map Key

- Mountain
- Desert
- Coniferous forest
- Deciduous forest
- Rain forest
- Grassland
- Wetland
- Tundra
- Ice cap

OCEAN

EUROPE

ALPS

Volga River

URAL MTS.

Europe-Asia boundary

Mediterranean Sea

AS. MTS.

SAHARA

AFRICA

Nile River

ASIA

Gobi

HIMALAYA

Yangtze River

PACIFIC OCEAN

EQUATOR

INDIAN OCEAN

AUSTRALIA

GREAT DIVIDING RANGE

ANTARCTICA

0   2000 miles

0   3000 kilometers

THE PHYSICAL WORLD CLOSE UP

The Earth's surface is made up of land and water. The biggest landmasses are called **continents.** All seven of them are named on this map. **Islands** are smaller pieces of land that are surrounded by water. Greenland is the largest island. Land that is almost entirely surrounded by water is called a **peninsula.** Europe has lots of them.

Oceans are the largest bodies of water. Can you find all four oceans? **Lakes** are bodies of water surrounded by land—like the Great Lakes, in North America. A large stream of water that flows into a lake or an ocean is called a **river.** The Nile is Earth's longest river.

These are Earth's main physical features. But continents also have mountains, deserts, forests, and many other kinds of physical features. The **map symbols** below show the features that will appear on the physical maps in this atlas. Each symbol is followed by a brief description that explains its meaning. There is also a photograph so you can see what each feature looks like in the real world.

Each continent has different kinds of features, so each physical map will have its own map key.

ARCTIC

GREENLAND

ROCKY MOUNTAINS

NORTH AMERICA

Great Lakes

APPALACHIAN MTS.

Mississippi River

ATLANTIC OCEAN

Gulf of Mexico

Caribbean Sea

PACIFIC OCEAN

EQUATOR

Amazon River

ANDES

SOUTH AMERICA

ANDES

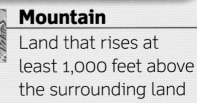
Mountain
Land that rises at least 1,000 feet above the surrounding land

Desert
Very dry land that can be hot or cold and sandy or rocky

Coniferous forest
Forest with trees that have seed cones and often needlelike leaves

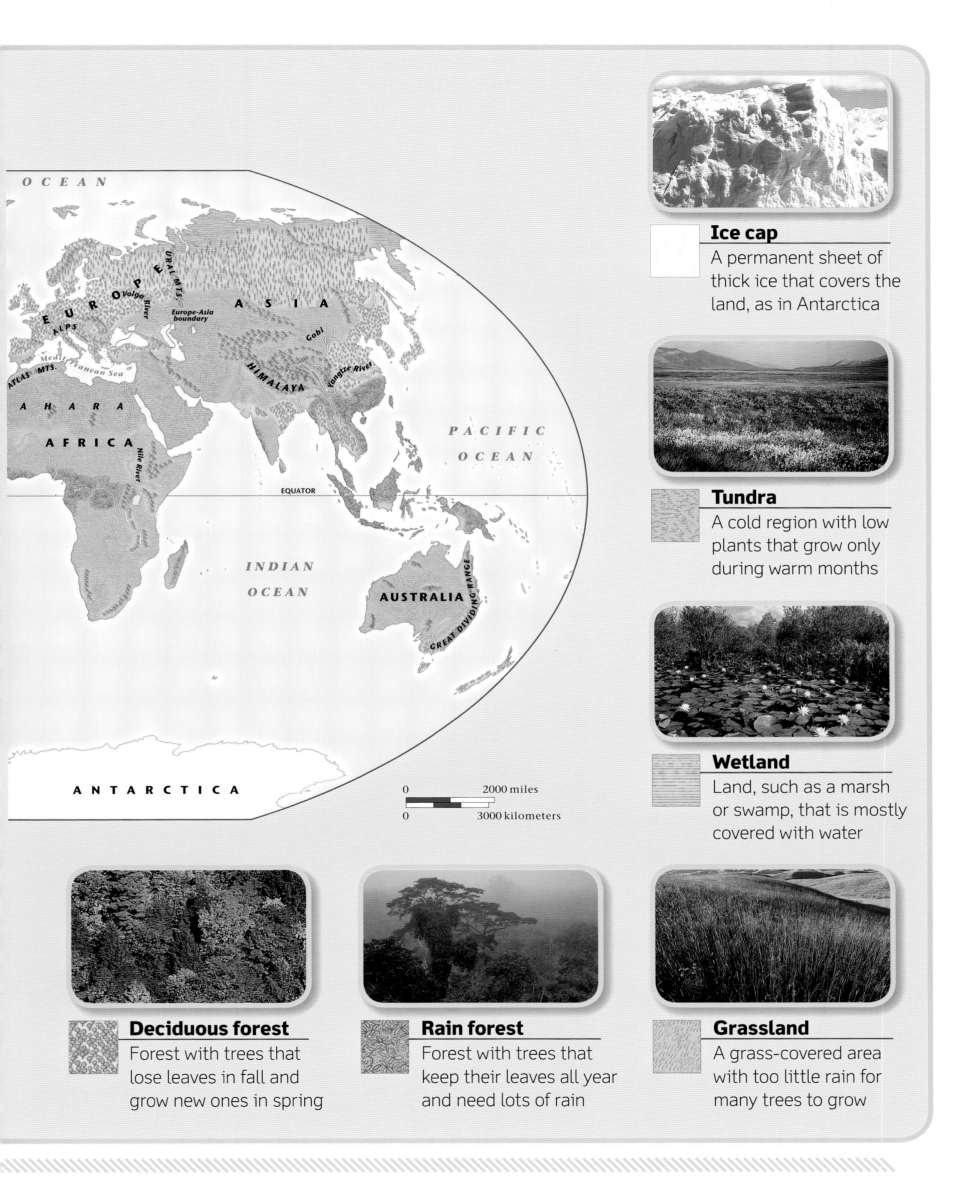

Ice cap
A permanent sheet of thick ice that covers the land, as in Antarctica

Tundra
A cold region with low plants that grow only during warm months

Wetland
Land, such as a marsh or swamp, that is mostly covered with water

Deciduous forest
Forest with trees that lose leaves in fall and grow new ones in spring

Rain forest
Forest with trees that keep their leaves all year and need lots of rain

Grassland
A grass-covered area with too little rain for many trees to grow

Map labels:
OCEAN
EUROPE
URAL MTS.
Volga River
Europe-Asia boundary
ALPS
ATLAS MTS.
Mediterranean Sea
SAHARA
AFRICA
Nile River
ASIA
Gobi
HIMALAYA
Yangtze River
PACIFIC OCEAN
EQUATOR
INDIAN OCEAN
AUSTRALIA
GREAT DIVIDING RANGE
ANTARCTICA

0   2000 miles
0   3000 kilometers

THE POLITICAL WORLD

Political maps show places where people live. This one names the countries of the world.

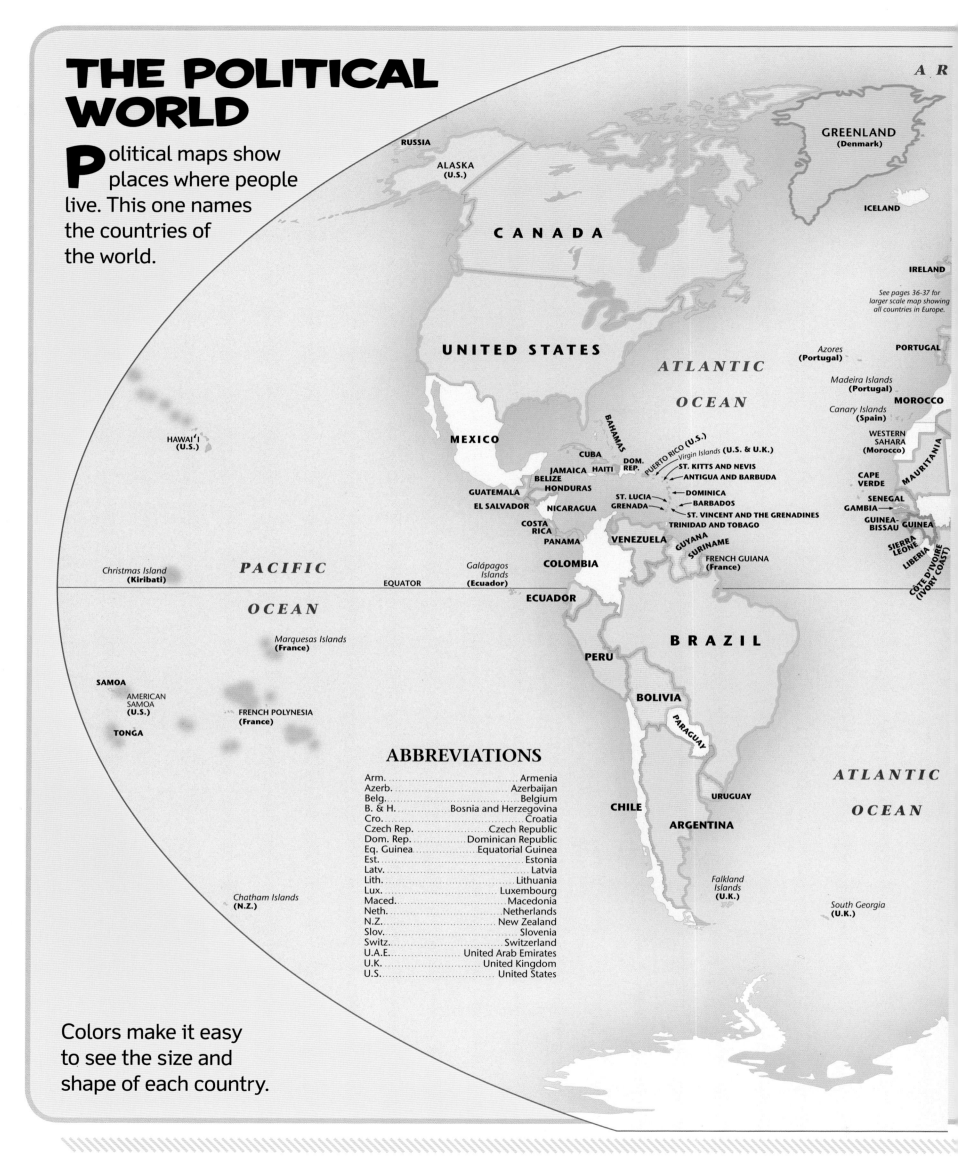

See pages 36-37 for larger scale map showing all countries in Europe.

ATLANTIC OCEAN

PACIFIC OCEAN

EQUATOR

Christmas Island (Kiribati)

Marquesas Islands (France)

SAMOA

AMERICAN SAMOA (U.S.)

FRENCH POLYNESIA (France)

TONGA

Chatham Islands (N.Z.)

RUSSIA

ALASKA (U.S.)

CANADA

UNITED STATES

HAWAI'I (U.S.)

MEXICO

GUATEMALA

EL SALVADOR

BELIZE

HONDURAS

NICARAGUA

COSTA RICA

PANAMA

CUBA

JAMAICA

HAITI

DOM. REP.

PUERTO RICO (U.S.)

BAHAMAS

Virgin Islands (U.S. & U.K.)

ST. KITTS AND NEVIS

ANTIGUA AND BARBUDA

DOMINICA

ST. LUCIA

BARBADOS

GRENADA

ST. VINCENT AND THE GRENADINES

TRINIDAD AND TOBAGO

VENEZUELA

COLOMBIA

GUYANA

SURINAME

FRENCH GUIANA (France)

ECUADOR

Galápagos Islands (Ecuador)

BRAZIL

PERU

BOLIVIA

PARAGUAY

CHILE

ARGENTINA

URUGUAY

Falkland Islands (U.K.)

South Georgia (U.K.)

GREENLAND (Denmark)

ICELAND

IRELAND

PORTUGAL

Azores (Portugal)

Madeira Islands (Portugal)

MOROCCO

Canary Islands (Spain)

WESTERN SAHARA (Morocco)

MAURITANIA

CAPE VERDE

SENEGAL

GAMBIA

GUINEA-BISSAU

GUINEA

SIERRA LEONE

LIBERIA

CÔTE D'IVOIRE (IVORY COAST)

ATLANTIC OCEAN

A R

ABBREVIATIONS

Arm.	Armenia
Azerb.	Azerbaijan
Belg.	Belgium
B. & H.	Bosnia and Herzegovina
Cro.	Croatia
Czech Rep.	Czech Republic
Dom. Rep.	Dominican Republic
Eq. Guinea	Equatorial Guinea
Est.	Estonia
Latv.	Latvia
Lith.	Lithuania
Lux.	Luxembourg
Maced.	Macedonia
Neth.	Netherlands
N.Z.	New Zealand
Slov.	Slovenia
Switz.	Switzerland
U.A.E.	United Arab Emirates
U.K.	United Kingdom
U.S.	United States

Colors make it easy to see the size and shape of each country.

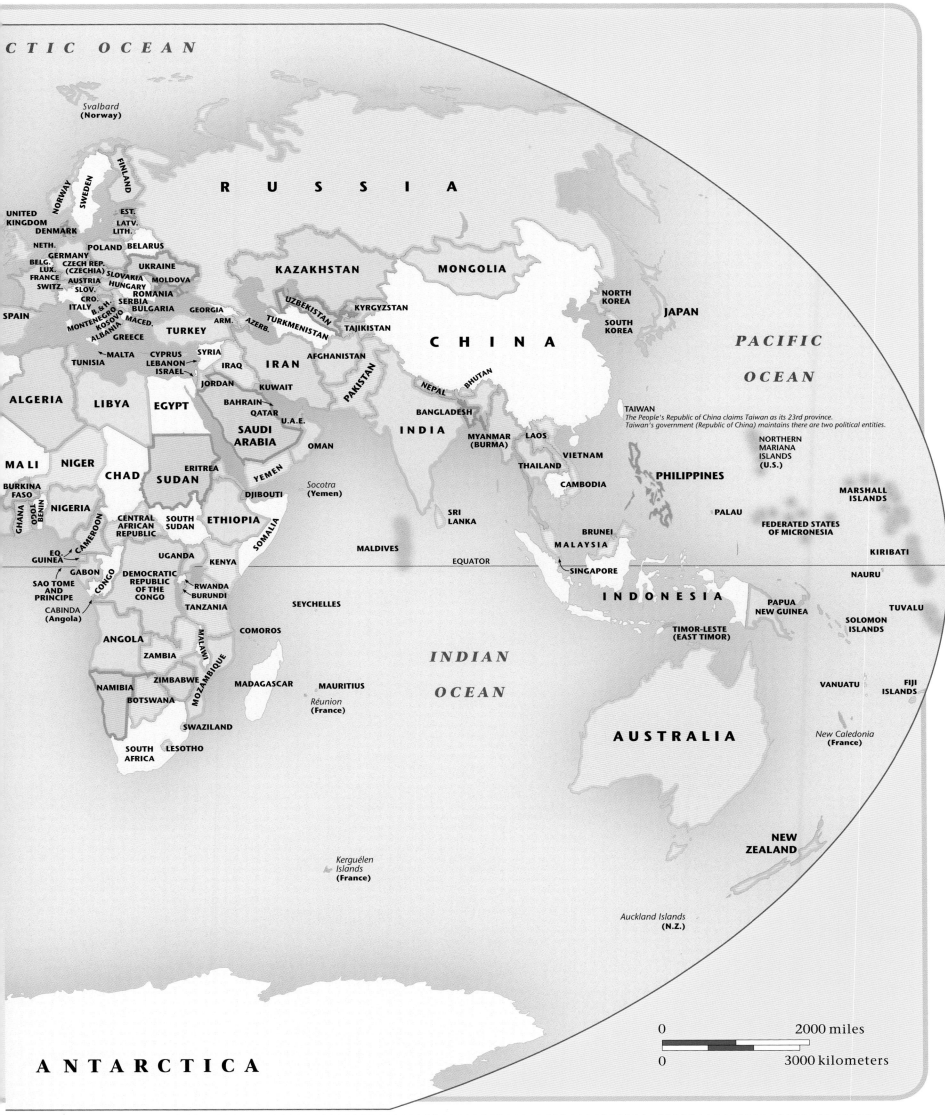

ARCTIC OCEAN

Svalbard
(Norway)

NORWAY
SWEDEN
FINLAND

UNITED
KINGDOM
DENMARK
EST.
LATV.
LITH.

NETH.
POLAND BELARUS
GERMANY
BELG.
LUX. CZECH REP.
FRANCE (CZECHIA) SLOVAKIA UKRAINE
SWITZ. AUSTRIA HUNGARY MOLDOVA
SLOV. ROMANIA
ITALY CRO. SERBIA
B.&H. BULGARIA GEORGIA
MONTENEGRO KOSOVO MACED. ARM. AZERB.
ALBANIA GREECE
SPAIN

RUSSIA

KAZAKHSTAN

MONGOLIA

NORTH
KOREA

JAPAN

PACIFIC

OCEAN

UZBEKISTAN KYRGYZSTAN
TURKMENISTAN TAJIKISTAN

SOUTH
KOREA

CHINA

TUNISIA
MALTA CYPRUS SYRIA
LEBANON
ISRAEL
JORDAN
IRAQ
IRAN AFGHANISTAN

NEPAL BHUTAN

TAIWAN
The People's Republic of China claims Taiwan as its 23rd province.
Taiwan's government (Republic of China) maintains there are two political entities.

ALGERIA LIBYA EGYPT
BAHRAIN
QATAR
U.A.E.
KUWAIT
SAUDI
ARABIA
OMAN

BANGLADESH

INDIA

MYANMAR
(BURMA) LAOS

PAKISTAN

NORTHERN
MARIANA
ISLANDS
(U.S.)

MALI NIGER CHAD
ERITREA
SUDAN
YEMEN
DJIBOUTI

Socotra
(Yemen)

THAILAND
VIETNAM

CAMBODIA

PHILIPPINES

MARSHALL
ISLANDS

BURKINA
FASO
NIGERIA
GHANA
TOGO
BENIN
CENTRAL
AFRICAN
REPUBLIC
SOUTH
SUDAN ETHIOPIA
SOMALIA

SRI
LANKA

MALDIVES

PALAU

FEDERATED STATES
OF MICRONESIA

KIRIBATI

EQ.
GUINEA CAMEROON
GABON
SAO TOME
AND
PRINCIPE
CABINDA
(Angola)
CONGO
UGANDA
DEMOCRATIC
REPUBLIC
OF THE
CONGO
RWANDA
BURUNDI
TANZANIA
KENYA

EQUATOR

BRUNEI
MALAYSIA
SINGAPORE

INDONESIA

NAURU

SEYCHELLES

PAPUA
NEW GUINEA

TUVALU

SOLOMON
ISLANDS

ANGOLA
ZAMBIA
NAMIBIA
BOTSWANA
ZIMBABWE
MALAWI
MOZAMBIQUE
SWAZILAND
SOUTH
AFRICA LESOTHO

COMOROS

MADAGASCAR

MAURITIUS

Réunion
(France)

INDIAN

OCEAN

TIMOR-LESTE
(EAST TIMOR)

VANUATU

FIJI
ISLANDS

AUSTRALIA

New Caledonia
(France)

Kerguélen
Islands
(France)

NEW
ZEALAND

Auckland Islands
(N.Z.)

0   2000 miles

0   3000 kilometers

ANTARCTICA

NORTH AMERICA

North America is shaped like a triangle. It is wide in the north. In the south it becomes a strip of land so narrow that a marathon runner could cross it in two hours. Ships make the trip on the Panama Canal. The warm islands in the Caribbean Sea are part of North America. So is icy Greenland in the far north. The seven countries between Mexico and South America make up a region commonly called Central America. It connects the rest of North America and South America.

Kha-hay! I'm from the Crow Tribe in Montana. This beautiful scene is the Grand Canyon, located in the state of Arizona. The mighty Colorado River runs through the canyon. Look for the river on the map when you turn the page.

NORTH AMERICA

Mt. McKinley
(Denali)
**Highest elevation in
North America**

ASIA

LAND REGIONS The Rocky Mountains run along the west side of North America through Mexico. In Mexico, the mountains are called the Sierra Madre Oriental. Lower mountains called the Appalachians are in the east. Grassy plains lie between the two mountains chains.

North America is famous for its **deciduous forests.** Leaves turn fiery colors each fall. ➔

WATER Together the Mississippi and the Missouri make up the longest river. The Great Lakes are the world's largest group of freshwater lakes.

A white-tailed deer nuzzles her babies in a meadow near the **Great Lakes.** Deer live in almost every country on the continent. ⬇

CLIMATE The far north is icy cold. Temperatures get warmer as you move south. Much of Central America is hot and wet.

PLANTS North America has large forests where there is plenty of rain. Grasslands cover drier areas.

◀ Palm trees grow along sandy beaches on islands in the **Caribbean Sea.** In this part of North America the weather is warm year-round.

ANIMALS There is a big variety of animals— everything from bears, moose, and wolves to monkeys and colorful parrots.

Deserts are found in the southwestern part of North America. The large rock formation on the right is called The Mitten. Can you guess why? ⬇

◀ Dragonlike iguanas live in the rain forests of **Mexico and Central America.** This harmless lizard can grow as long as a man's leg.

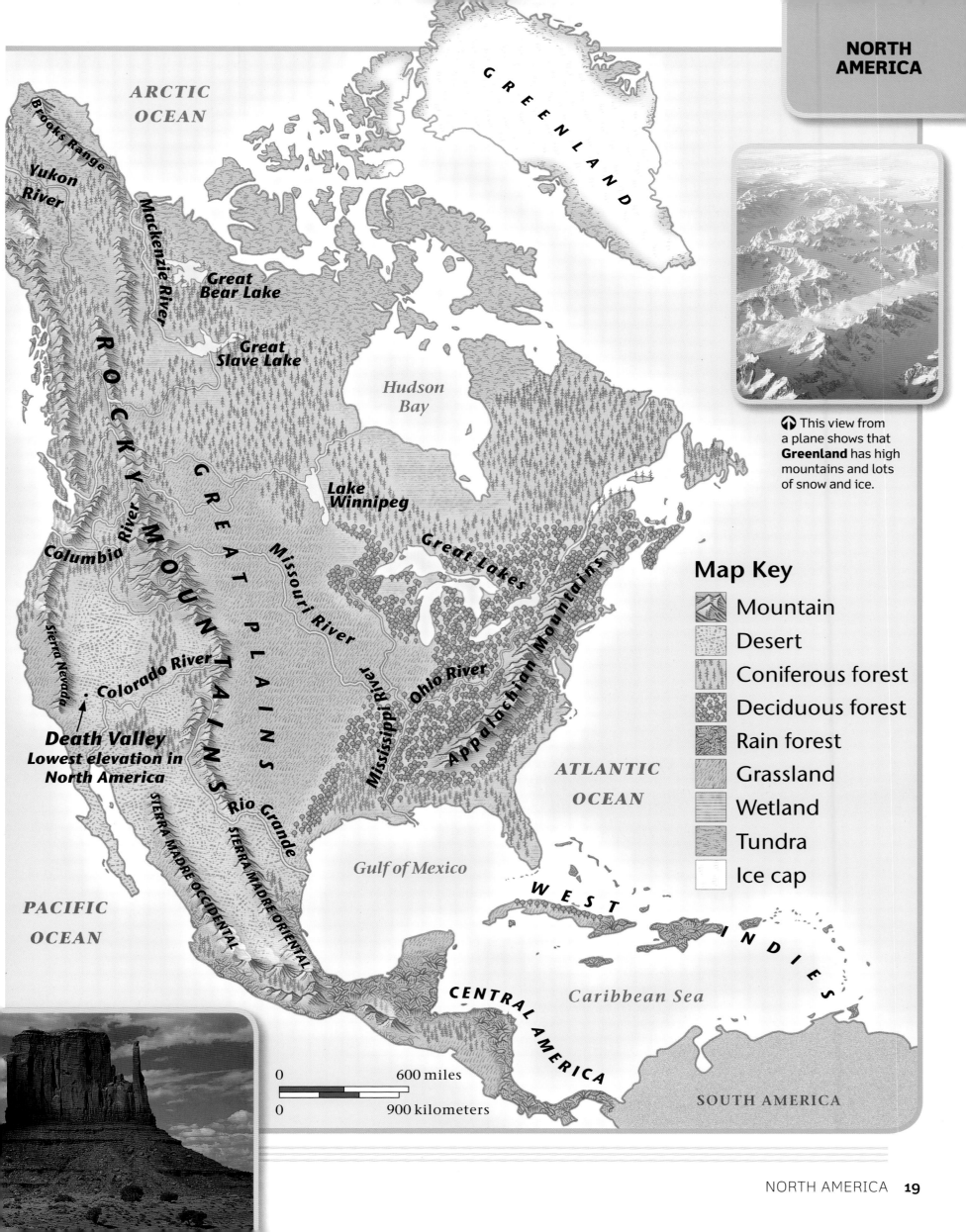

ARCTIC OCEAN

G R E E N L A N D

Brooks Range

Yukon River

Mackenzie River

Great Bear Lake

Great Slave Lake

Hudson Bay

Lake Winnipeg

R O C K Y   M O U N T A I N S

Columbia River

Sierra Nevada

Colorado River

Death Valley
Lowest elevation in North America

G R E A T   P L A I N S

Missouri River

Mississippi River

Great Lakes

Ohio River

Appalachian Mountains

SIERRA MADRE OCCIDENTAL

SIERRA MADRE ORIENTAL

Rio Grande

Gulf of Mexico

ATLANTIC OCEAN

PACIFIC OCEAN

W E S T   I N D I E S

CENTRAL AMERICA

Caribbean Sea

SOUTH AMERICA

This view from a plane shows that **Greenland** has high mountains and lots of snow and ice.

Map Key

- Mountain
- Desert
- Coniferous forest
- Deciduous forest
- Rain forest
- Grassland
- Wetland
- Tundra
- Ice cap

0   600 miles

0   900 kilometers

NORTH AMERICA

ASIA

ALASKA
(United States)

COUNTRIES Canada, the United States, Mexico, and the countries of Central America and the West Indies make up North America.

CITIES Mexico City is the biggest city in North America. Next in size are New York City and Los Angeles. Santo Domingo, in the Dominican Republic, is the largest city in the West Indies.

PEOPLE Ancestors of most people in North America came from Europe. Many other people trace their roots to Africa and Asia. Native Americans live throughout the continent.

LANGUAGES English and Spanish are the main languages. A large number of people in Canada and Haiti speak French. There are also many Native American languages.

PRODUCTS North America's chief products include cars, machinery, petroleum, natural gas, silver, wheat, corn, beef, and forest products.

⬆ Skiing and ski jumping are popular sports in the **Rocky Mountains.**

This farmer is harvesting wheat on a big farm in **Canada.** Canada and the United States grow much of the world's wheat. ➡

⬆ This is **Mexico City.** More people live here than in any other city in North America.

⬆ This pyramid at **Chichén Itzá,** in Mexico, was built long ago by the Maya people.

⬅ These red berries hold coffee beans. Many farmers in **Guatemala** make a living growing coffee.

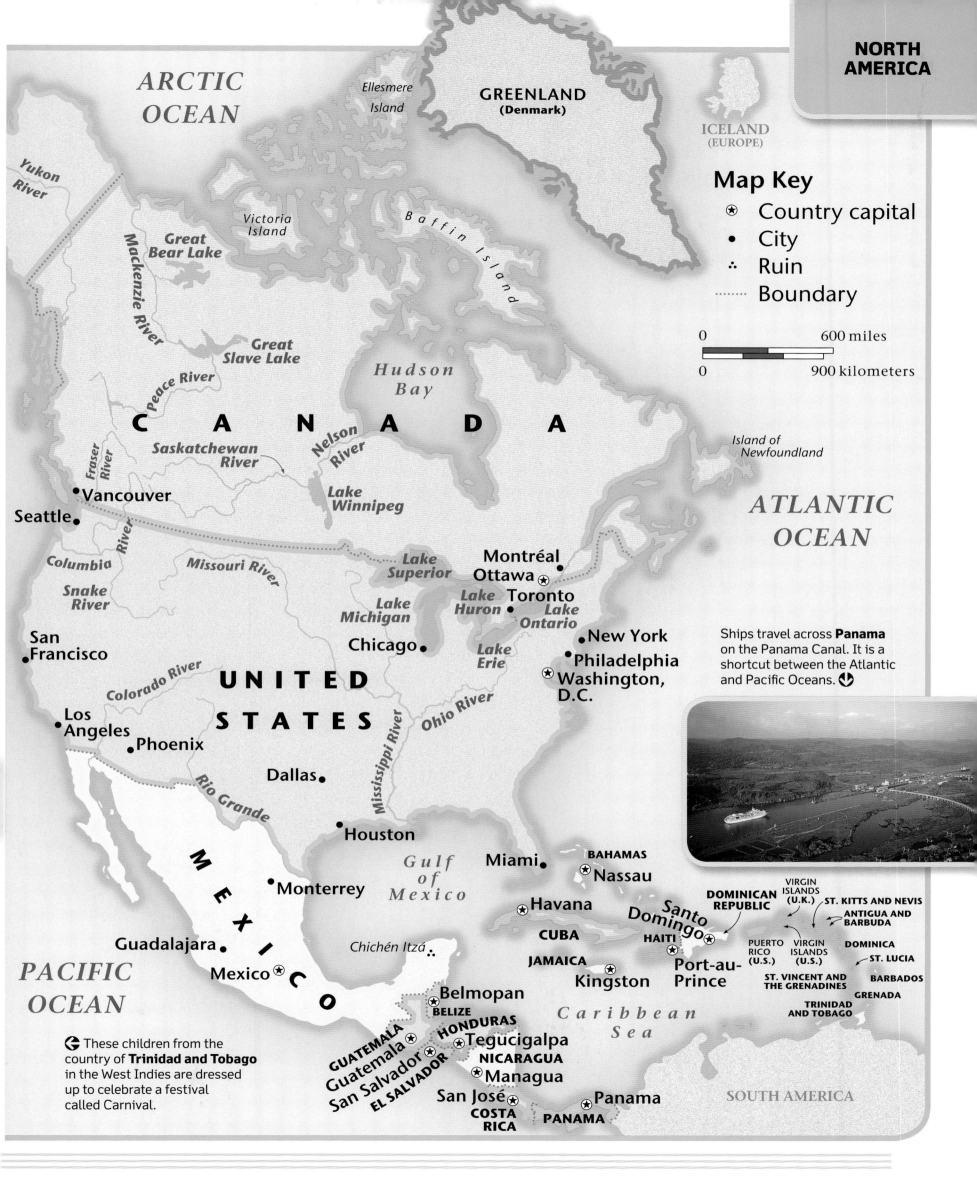

ARCTIC OCEAN

Yukon River

Ellesmere Island

GREENLAND (Denmark)

ICELAND (EUROPE)

Victoria Island

Great Bear Lake

Baffin Island

Mackenzie River

Peace River

Great Slave Lake

Hudson Bay

Map Key

⊛ Country capital

• City

∴ Ruin

⋯⋯ Boundary

| 0 | | 600 miles |

| 0 | | 900 kilometers |

C A N A D A

Saskatchewan River

Nelson River

Fraser River

Island of Newfoundland

ATLANTIC OCEAN

Vancouver

Seattle

Lake Winnipeg

Columbia River

Snake River

Missouri River

Lake Superior

Montréal
Ottawa ⊛
Lake Huron Toronto
Lake Michigan Lake Ontario

San Francisco

Chicago

Lake Erie

New York
Philadelphia
⊛ Washington, D.C.

Ships travel across **Panama** on the Panama Canal. It is a shortcut between the Atlantic and Pacific Oceans. ⬇

U N I T E D   S T A T E S

Colorado River

Los Angeles

Phoenix

Mississippi River

Ohio River

Dallas

Rio Grande

Houston

Monterrey

Gulf of Mexico

Miami

BAHAMAS
⊛ Nassau

M E X I C O

Havana ⊛

CUBA

Santo Domingo
DOMINICAN REPUBLIC
HAITI ⊛

VIRGIN ISLANDS (U.K.)
ST. KITTS AND NEVIS
ANTIGUA AND BARBUDA

PUERTO RICO (U.S.)
VIRGIN ISLANDS (U.S.)
DOMINICA

Guadalajara

Chichén Itzá

JAMAICA

ST. LUCIA

PACIFIC OCEAN

Mexico ⊛

Kingston

Port-au-Prince ⊛

ST. VINCENT AND THE GRENADINES

BARBADOS

GRENADA

Belmopan ⊛
BELIZE

Caribbean Sea

TRINIDAD AND TOBAGO

⟲ These children from the country of **Trinidad and Tobago** in the West Indies are dressed up to celebrate a festival called Carnival.

GUATEMALA ⊛
Guatemala
San Salvador ⊛
EL SALVADOR

HONDURAS
Tegucigalpa ⊛

NICARAGUA
⊛ Managua

San José ⊛
COSTA RICA
PANAMA

⊛ Panama

SOUTH AMERICA

UNITED STATES

 STATES The United States is made up of 50 states. Alaska and Hawai'i are separated from the rest of the country. So you can see them close up, they are shown near the bottom of the map. Use the small globe above to see their real locations.

 CITIES Washington, D.C., is the national capital. Each state also has a capital city. New York City has the most people.

 PEOPLE People from almost every country in the world live in the United States. Most live and work in and around cities.

 LANGUAGES English is the chief language, followed by Spanish.

 PRODUCTS The chief products include cars, machinery, petroleum, natural gas, coal, beef, wheat, and forest products.

Baseball is a popular sport in the **United States** along with soccer, basketball, and football. This girl is getting ready to swing her bat at a baseball game.➔

⬆ Sandy beaches, like this one in **Delaware,** are popular places to visit in the summer.

⬆ Chinese New Year is a big celebration in **San Francisco.** Lots of Chinese live there.

Seattle
Olympia
Portland
Salem
WASHINGTON
Columbia River
OREGON
IDAHO
Boise
Helena
M
Carson City
Sacramento
San Francisco
San Jose
NEVADA
Salt Lake City
UTAH
Colorado
Las Vegas
Los Angeles
ARIZONA
Phoenix
San Diego
Tucson

CALIFORNIA

PACIFIC OCEAN

ALASKA
Juneau

0   400 miles
0   600 kilometers

Honolulu
HAWAI'I

0   150 miles
0   200 kilometers

CANADA

Missouri River

MONTANA

NORTH DAKOTA
· Bismarck

MINNESOTA

Lake Superior

M I C H I G A N

L. Huron

MAINE
· Augusta

Montpelier
VT.
N.H.
· Concord

SOUTH DAKOTA
· Pierre

Minneapolis ⊙ St. Paul
WISCONSIN
Milwaukee ·
Madison ⊙

NEW YORK

Rochester ·
Albany ⊙

Lake Ontario

Boston ·
MASS.
· Providence
Hartford ⊙
CONN.
RHODE ISLAND

WYOMING

· Lansing

L. Michigan

Detroit ·

L. Erie

Buffalo ·

ATLANTIC OCEAN

Cheyenne ⊙

NEBRASKA

I O W A
Des Moines ⊙

Chicago ·

Cleveland ·
Pittsburgh ·

PENNSYLVANIA
Harrisburg ⊙

Trenton ⊙
NEW JERSEY

New York ·

River

Omaha ·
Lincoln ⊙

ILLINOIS

INDIANA

O H I O

Baltimore ·
MARYLAND

Philadelphia ·
Dover ⊙
DELAWARE

Denver ⊙
COLORADO

Springfield ⊙

Indianapolis ⊙

Columbus ⊙
WEST VIRGINIA

Washington, D.C. ⊛ Annapolis ⊙

This bridge is in **New York City.** The Empire State Building stands tall against the sky. ⬇

Topeka ⊙
K A N S A S

Kansas City ·
Jefferson City ⊙

St. Louis ·

Cincinnati ·

Charleston ⊙

Richmond ⊙

Wichita ·

MISSOURI

Frankfort ⊙

VIRGINIA

K E N T U C K Y

Raleigh ⊙

Santa Fe ⊙

Tulsa ·
OKLAHOMA

Nashville ⊙

T E N N E S S E E

NORTH CAROLINA
· Charlotte

Albuquerque ·

Oklahoma City ⊙

ARKANSAS

Memphis ·

SOUTH

⊙ Columbia
CAROLINA

NEW MEXICO

Little ⊙ Rock

Mississippi River

Atlanta ⊙

· El Paso

Dallas ·

MISSISSIPPI

· Birmingham
ALABAMA
GEORGIA

· Savannah

Fort Worth ·

Jackson ⊙

· Montgomery

T E X A S

LOUISIANA

Jacksonville ·

Austin ⊙

Tallahassee ⊙

F L O R I D A

Rio Grande

Baton ⊙ Rouge
· New Orleans

Houston ·
San Antonio ·

Orlando ⊙

Gulf of Mexico

Tampa ·

MEXICO

Map Key

⊛ Country capital

⊙ State capital

· City

⋯⋯ Boundary

0   400 miles

0   600 kilometers

· Miami

A scarecrow stands guard over a field of sunflowers in **Kansas.** ⬇

Spicy boiled crawfish are a favorite dish in **Mississippi** and other states that border the Gulf of Mexico. ➡

CANADA

PROVINCES Canada is divided into ten provinces and three territories. Nunavut is a brand-new homeland for Eskimos. The largest number of people live in Ontario and Quebec.

CITIES Ottawa is Canada's capital. Toronto, Montréal, and Vancouver are among its largest cities and ports.

PEOPLE Canada has fewer people than the state of California. Most Canadians live within a hundred miles of the country's southern border. The territories have a lot of land but very few people.

LANGUAGES Canada's street signs are often in two languages. That's because English and French are the chief languages. Most French-speaking Canadians live in Quebec.

PRODUCTS Canada's chief products include cars, forest products, petroleum, natural gas, aluminum, nickel, iron ore, beef, and wheat.

↢ Royal Canadian Mounted Police often perform their famous Musical Ride in **Ottawa.**

ARCTIC

Beaufort Sea

ALASKA (U.S.)

YUKON TERRITORY

Mackenzie River

Yukon River

⊙ **Whitehorse**

NORTHWEST TERRITORIES

BRITISH COLUMBIA

Peace River

ALBERTA

Edmonton ⊙

Fraser River

Vancouver Island

Victoria ⊙

•**Vancouver**

Calgary ⊙

⚓ Banff, in **Alberta,** is one of several national parks in the Rocky Mountains of western Canada.

PACIFIC OCEAN

↢ During Canada's long, cold winters, ice hockey is a popular sport. The Hockey Hall of Fame is in **Toronto,** Ontario.

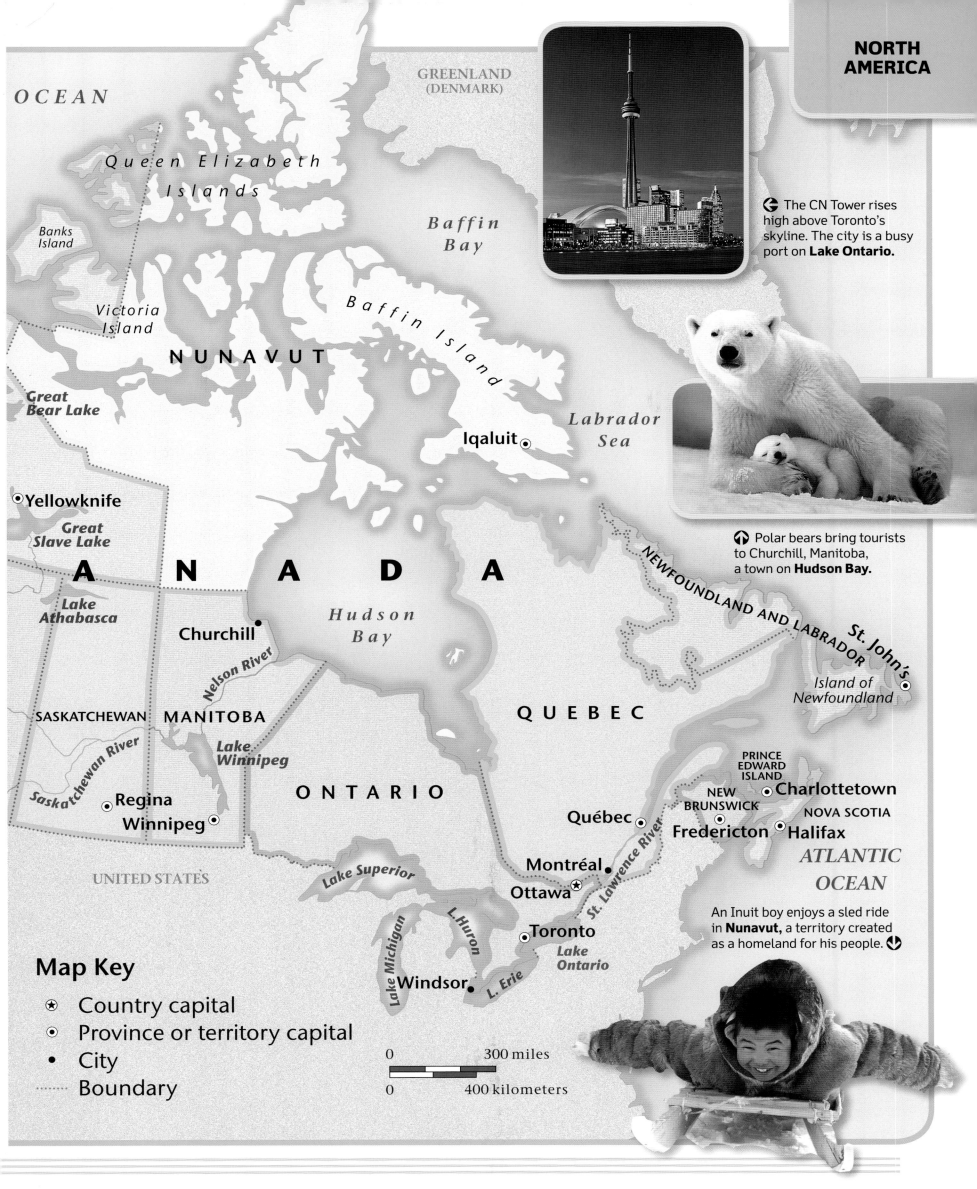

OCEAN

GREENLAND (DENMARK)

Queen Elizabeth Islands

Baffin Bay

Banks Island

Victoria Island

NUNAVUT

Baffin Island

Labrador Sea

Great Bear Lake

Iqaluit

The CN Tower rises high above Toronto's skyline. The city is a busy port on **Lake Ontario.**

Yellowknife

Great Slave Lake

C A N A D A

Polar bears bring tourists to Churchill, Manitoba, a town on **Hudson Bay.**

Lake Athabasca

Churchill

Hudson Bay

NEWFOUNDLAND AND LABRADOR

St. John's

Nelson River

SASKATCHEWAN   **MANITOBA**

Saskatchewan River

Lake Winnipeg

QUEBEC

Island of Newfoundland

PRINCE EDWARD ISLAND

ONTARIO

Regina
Winnipeg

NEW BRUNSWICK

Charlottetown

NOVA SCOTIA

Québec

Fredericton   Halifax

UNITED STATES

Lake Superior

Montréal

St. Lawrence River

ATLANTIC OCEAN

Ottawa

L. Huron

Lake Michigan

Toronto

Lake Ontario

An Inuit boy enjoys a sled ride in **Nunavut,** a territory created as a homeland for his people.

Windsor   *L. Erie*

Map Key

⊛ Country capital

⊙ Province or territory capital

• City

⋯⋯ Boundary

0 ———— 300 miles

0 ———— 400 kilometers

SOUTH AMERICA

Visit South America and you will see many wonderful things. It has the world's biggest rain forest and one of the driest deserts. It has emerald mines, mysterious ruins, and crowded modern cities with glass-and-steel skyscrapers. In the mountains, camel-like animals called llamas are trained to carry goods. On the grasslands, cowboys called gauchos round up cattle. You might be surprised to learn that some familiar foods, such as potatoes and tomatoes, are native to South America.

Imaynalla! Greetings in Quechua, my native language. I live in Peru. Do you like my market-day outfit? Behind me is Machu Picchu, an ancient Inca city located high in the Andes mountains of my country.

SOUTH AMERICA

 LAND REGIONS Snowcapped mountains called the Andes run along the west coast. Rain forests and grasslands cover much of the rest of the continent. The continent's driest desert lies between the Andes and the Pacific Ocean.

 WATER The Amazon River carries more water than any other river in the world. More than 1,000 streams and rivers flow into it. Lake Titicaca, in the Andes, is the continent's largest lake.

 CLIMATE Much of South America is warm all year. The coldest places are in the Andes and at the continent's southern tip. Each year about 80 inches of rain falls in the rain forests.

 PLANTS The Amazon rain forest has more kinds of plants than any other place in the world. Grasslands feed large herds of cattle and sheep.

ANIMALS Colorful macaws, noisy howler monkeys, and giant snakes live in the rain forest. Sure-footed llamas, huge birds called condors, and guinea pigs live in the Andes. The flightless rhea, which looks like an ostrich, roams the wide southern grasslands.

← Imagine living in a place where birds are as big and as colorful as these macaws. They live in the **rain forest.**

⬆ The **Atacama,** in northern Chile, is one of the world's driest deserts.

⬆ Llamas are camel-like animals that live in the **Andes.**

The world's largest water lilies grow in the **Amazon River.** They are big enough to hold a kid. ➔

Cold outside and hot inside, snow-covered **volcanoes** are scattered throughout the Andes. ➔

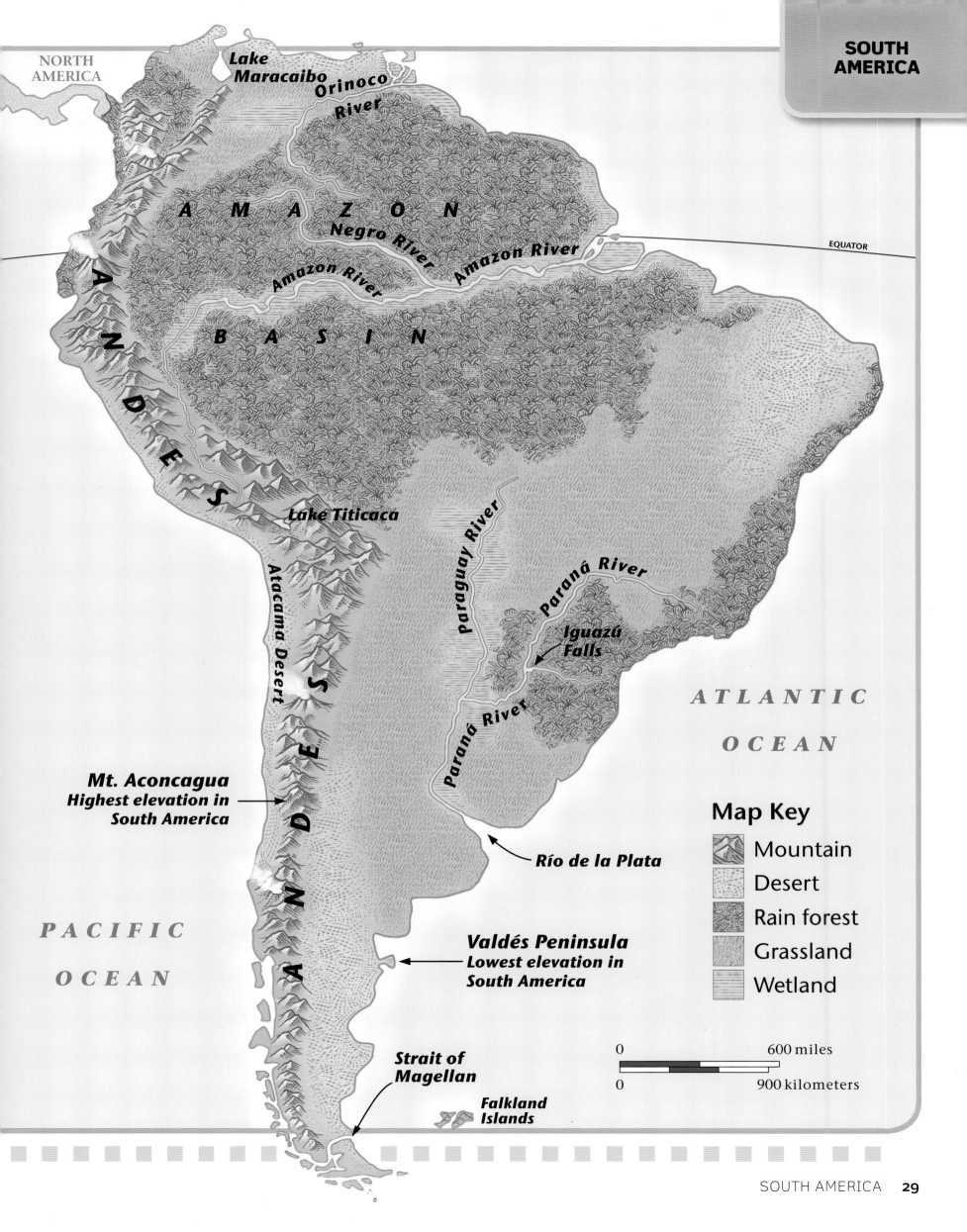

NORTH AMERICA

Lake Maracaibo

Orinoco River

A M A Z O N

Negro River

Amazon River

Amazon River

EQUATOR

A N D E S

B A S I N

Lake Titicaca

Paraguay River

Paraná River

Iguazú Falls

Atacama Desert

A N D E S

Paraná River

Paraná River

ATLANTIC OCEAN

Mt. Aconcagua
Highest elevation in South America

Río de la Plata

PACIFIC OCEAN

Valdés Peninsula
Lowest elevation in South America

Map Key

Mountain
Desert
Rain forest
Grassland
Wetland

0   600 miles

0   900 kilometers

Strait of Magellan

Falkland Islands

SOUTH AMERICA

↑ Many religious festivals take place all over **South America.** Here, a girl is dancing as she celebrates a Catholic fiesta.

 COUNTRIES South America has just 12 countries—French Guiana is not really a country because it belongs to France. All but two of these countries border an ocean. Can you find these two countries on the map?

 CITIES Most of the largest cities are near the oceans. São Paulo, in Brazil, is South America's biggest city. Bolivia has two capital cities: La Paz and Sucre.

PEOPLE The native people came from the north long ago. Colonists came from Europe, especially from Spain and Portugal. They brought African slaves to work in the fields. Most people in South America are descendants of these three groups.

 LANGUAGES Spanish and Portuguese are the continent's chief languages. Indians speak Quechua and other native languages.

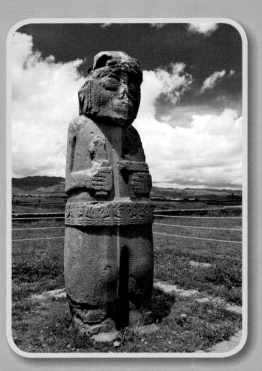

← This statue was carved from stone during the Tiwanaku civilization. These ancient peoples lived near Lake Titicaca in **Bolivia.**

These unpolished stones are emeralds. **Colombia** is the top producer of these gems. ↓

 PRODUCTS South America's chief products include bananas, cattle, coffee, copper, emeralds, oranges, and sugar.

← This man plays his guitar to entertain people on the streets of **Buenos Aires,** in Argentina. Guitar music is popular in South America.

← Soccer is the most popular sport in South America. This player from **Brazil** is focused on scoring a goal.

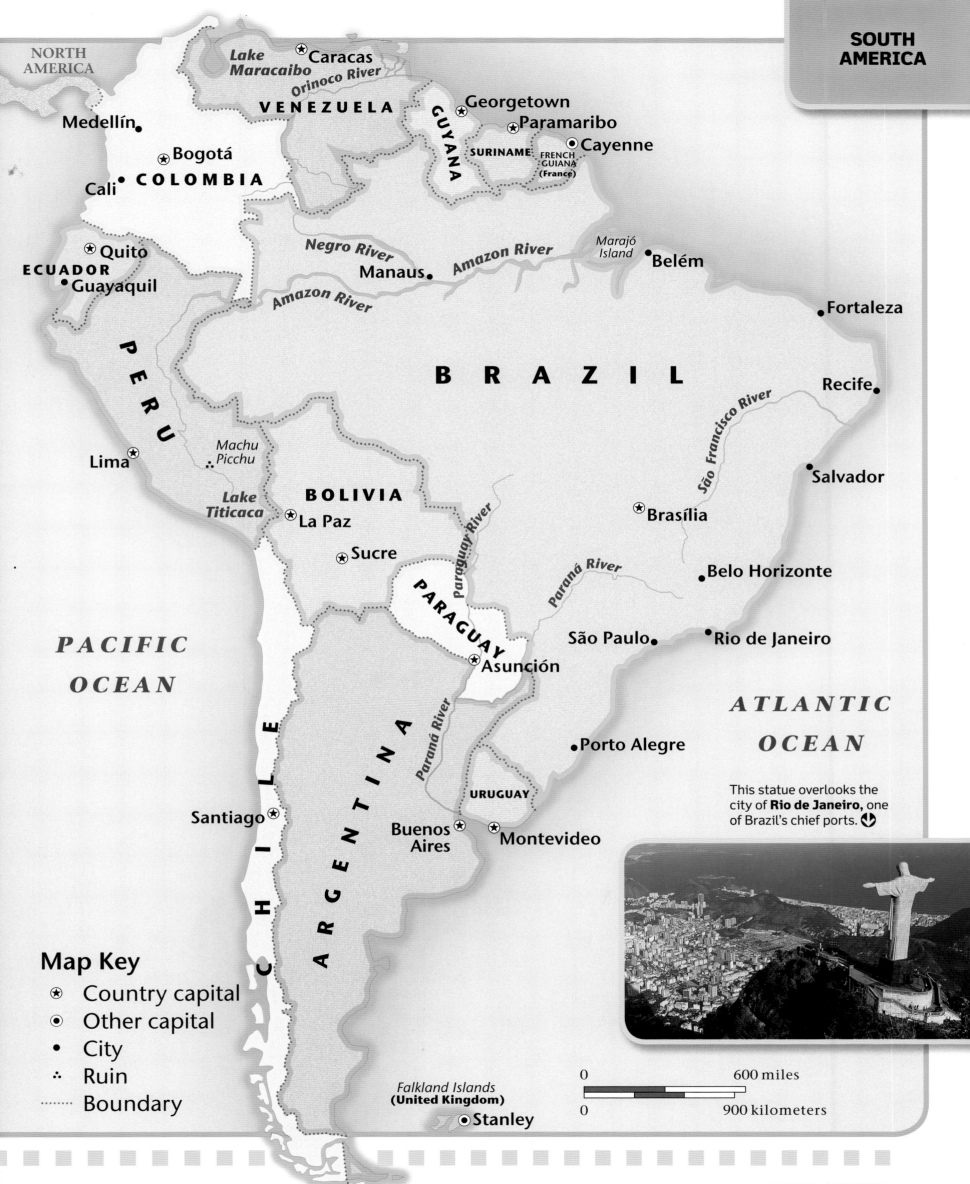

NORTH
AMERICA

Lake
Maracaibo

⊛ Caracas

Orinoco River

Georgetown ⊙

Paramaribo ⊙

VENEZUELA

GUYANA

SURINAME

Cayenne ⊙

Medellín •

FRENCH
GUIANA
(France)

⊛ Bogotá

COLOMBIA

Cali •

⊛ Quito

ECUADOR

• Guayaquil

Negro River

Amazon River

Marajó
Island

• Belém

Manaus •

Amazon River

• Fortaleza

B R A Z I L

Recife •

P
E
R
U

Machu
Picchu ∴

São Francisco River

Lima ⊛

Salvador •

Lake
Titicaca

BOLIVIA

⊛ La Paz

⊛ Brasília

⊛ Sucre

Paraguay River

Belo Horizonte •

Paraná River

PACIFIC

PARAGUAY

São Paulo •

• Rio de Janeiro

OCEAN

⊛ Asunción

ATLANTIC

Paraná River

OCEAN

C
H
I
L
E

A
R
G
E
N
T
I
N
A

• Porto Alegre

This statue overlooks the
city of **Rio de Janeiro**, one
of Brazil's chief ports. ⬇

URUGUAY

Santiago ⊛

Buenos
Aires ⊛

⊛ Montevideo

Map Key

⊛ Country capital

⊙ Other capital

• City

∴ Ruin

•••• Boundary

Falkland Islands
(United Kingdom)

0   600 miles

0   900 kilometers

⊙ Stanley

EUROPE

Travel through the countryside in Europe and you might think you have wandered into the pages of a storybook. You'll see castles, cuckoo clocks, and cobblestone streets. But Europe is also one of the most modern continents. You can ride one of the world's fastest trains through a tunnel beneath the English Channel, watch sports cars being made in Italy, and visit famous museums in Paris. On a map Europe may look like it is part of Asia, but it is considered to be a separate continent.

Sveiks! I'm from Latvia, a country on the Baltic Sea. I am wearing a costume for a dance. This is the Louvre in Paris, France. It is one of the most famous museums in the world, and home of the "Mona Lisa."

EUROPE

LAND REGIONS
Europe's most obvious feature is its coastline, cut with bays and peninsulas of every size. The Alps are high mountains that form a chain across much of southern Europe.

WATER
Several large rivers flow across Europe. Some of the most important include the Danube, Rhine, Volga, and Rhône.

CLIMATE
Warm winds from the Atlantic Ocean help give most of Europe a mild climate. This climate plus plenty of rain makes much of Europe good for farming.

PLANTS
Europe's largest forests are in the north. Cork and olive trees grow along the Mediterranean Sea.

ANIMALS
Reindeer are common in the far north. Many kinds of goatlike animals live in the Alps. Robins, nightingales, and sparrows are among Europe's native birds.

⬅ European rabbits live all over the **continent.**

⬅ People often try to climb the **Matterhorn.** It is one of the highest peaks in the Alps.

⬆ Much of Europe is farmland. Fields of lavender grow in the mild climate east of the **Rhône.** Perfume is made from these flowers.

Iceland

ATLANTIC OCEAN

Ireland

Great Britain

PYRENEES

IBERIAN PENINSULA

Me

AFRICA

⬅ This is a kind of wild goat called an ibex. It is one of many kinds of hooved animals that live in the **Alps** and other mountainous parts of the continent.

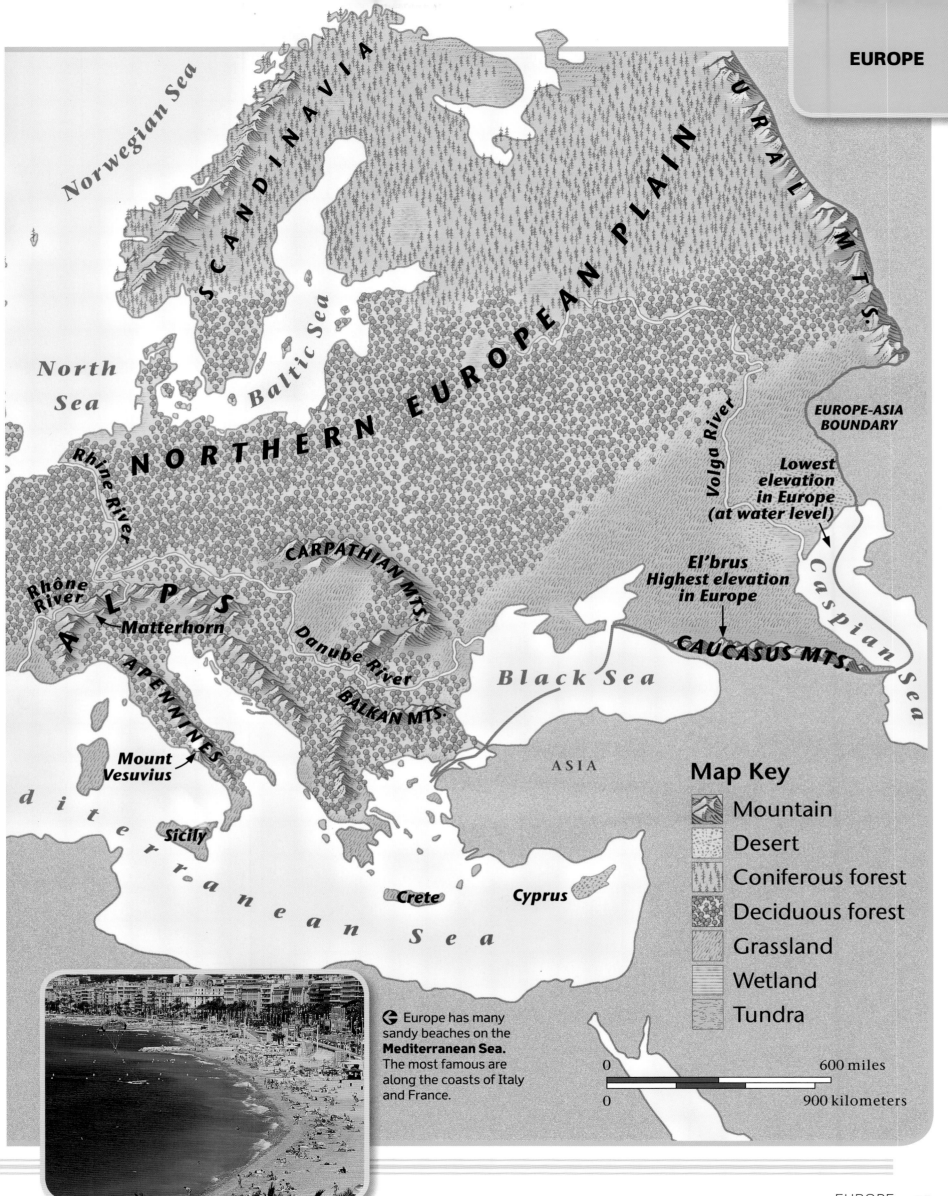

Norwegian Sea

SCANDINAVIA

URAL MTS.

North Sea

Baltic Sea

NORTHERN EUROPEAN PLAIN

Volga River

EUROPE-ASIA BOUNDARY

Rhine River

Lowest elevation in Europe (at water level)

CARPATHIAN MTS.

Rhône River

A L P S

Matterhorn

Danube River

El'brus Highest elevation in Europe

CAUCASUS MTS.

Caspian Sea

BALKAN MTS.

Black Sea

APENNINES

Mount Vesuvius

ASIA

M e d i t e r r a n e a n   S e a

Sicily

Crete

Cyprus

Map Key

Mountain

Desert

Coniferous forest

Deciduous forest

Grassland

Wetland

Tundra

Europe has many sandy beaches on the **Mediterranean Sea.** The most famous are along the coasts of Italy and France.

0   600 miles

0   900 kilometers

EUROPE

St. Basil's is a famous Russian orthodox church. It is in **Moscow,** Russia's capital city.

COUNTRIES There are 46 countries in Europe. Even though most of Russia is in Asia *(see pages 42–43),* the country is usually counted as being part of Europe. There are five island countries: Iceland, the United Kingdom, Ireland, Malta, and Cyprus.

CITIES Most cities in Europe are within a few hundred miles of the sea. London, in the United Kingdom, is Europe's largest city.

PEOPLE There are many different ethnic groups in Europe—usually one main group for each country. More people live in cities than on farms.

LANGUAGES About 50 languages are spoken in Europe, including English, French, German, and Russian. Many Europeans speak more than one language.

PRODUCTS Europe's chief products include iron, coal, petroleum, cars, machinery, wheat, fruit, and olives.

Inspectors examine cheese at a market in the **Netherlands.** Europe is famous for its cheeses.

The euro is currently the official money in **Greece** and 16 other members of the European Union *(see page 61).*

Bagpipe music is popular in Scotland, which was once an independent country. Today, Scotland is part of the **United Kingdom.**

Reykjavík **ICELAND**

ATLANTIC OCEAN

Faroe Islands **(Denmark)**

Orkney Islands

Edinburgh

IRELAND **UNITED**
Dublin **KINGDOM**

London

English Channel

FRA

Bordeaux

PORTUGAL

ANDORRA

Lisbon

Madrid

SPAIN

Seville

Balearic Islands **(Spain)**

GIBRALTAR (U.K)

AFRICA

Norwegian Sea

Shetland Islands

N O R W A Y

S W E D E N

F I N L A N D

Oslo ⊛

Helsinki ⊛

• St. Petersburg

North Sea

Stockholm ⊛

⊛ Tallinn
ESTONIA

R U S S I A

Map Key

⊛ Country capital

• City

...... Boundary

0		600 miles
0		900 kilometers

Baltic Sea

Riga ⊛

LATVIA

DENMARK
Copenhagen ⊛

LITHUANIA

⊛ Vilnius

⊛ Moscow

KALININGRAD
(Russia)

⊛ Minsk

Volga River

NETHERLANDS
⊛ Amsterdam

• Hamburg

Berlin ⊛

B E L A R U S

KAZAKHSTAN

Brussels ⊛
BELGIUM

GERMANY

Warsaw ⊛

P O L A N D

Volgograd •

Paris •

Rhine River

LUXEMBOURG

Prague ⊛

• Cracow

⊛ Kiev

U K R A I N E

Caspian Sea

**CZECH REPUBLIC
(CZECHIA)**

Danube River

N C E

Vienna ⊛

SLOVAKIA

⊛ Bratislava

MOLDOVA

Bern ⊛

LIECHTENSTEIN

AUSTRIA

⊛ Budapest

Chisinau ⊛

⊛ Tbilisi

Baku ⊛

GEORGIA

SWITZERLAND

SLOVENIA

HUNGARY

Ljubljana ⊛

⊛ Zagreb

ROMANIA

AZERBAIJAN

Rhone R.

CROATIA

SAN MARINO

Belgrade ⊛

• Bucharest ⊛

MONACO

**BOSNIA AND
HERZEGOVINA**

Danube River

Black Sea

*Corsica
(France)*

Sarajevo ⊛

SERBIA

ITALY

MONTENEGRO

KOSOVO

Prishtina ⊛

BULGARIA

**VATICAN
CITY**

⊛ Rome

Podgorica ⊛

⊛ Sofia

• Skopje

*Sardinia
(Italy)*

• Naples

Tirana ⊛

MACEDONIA

ALBANIA

G R E E C E

Istanbul •

⊛ Ankara

T U R K E Y

Sicily

⊛ Athens

NOTE: The countries of Turkey, Georgia, Azerbaijan, Kazakhstan, and Russia are in both the continents of Europe and Asia.

M e d i t e r r a n e a n   S e a

⊛ Valletta

MALTA

Crete

Nicosia ⊛

CYPRUS

A S I A

A S I A

⊖ The Colosseum lights up as the sun begins to set in **Rome**, Italy. This amphitheater was built by the Roman Empire almost 2,000 years ago.

⊖ These girls are dressed for a festival in **Spain**. Such celebrations keep folk traditions alive.

ASIA

Asia is Earth's largest continent. Mount Everest, the world's highest mountain, is here. Asia also has some of the world's longest rivers, biggest deserts, and thickest forests. The Dead Sea is the lowest place on the continent. It is called "dead" because its water is too salty for fish and other animals to live in. More people live in Asia than anywhere else. The world's very first cities were built along river valleys in Asia long, long ago.

Namaste, I'm from India. My country is home to the Taj Mahal, a famous tomb built hundreds of years ago. The bright lights and colorful signs behind me are in the lively city of Tokyo, Japan. Tokyo is the most populous city in the world.

ASIA

LAND REGIONS

Much of Asia is a rolling plain covered by grasslands, forests, and tundra. The Himalaya and other high mountains stretch across the south. Deserts cover much of southwestern and central Asia.

WATER

Asia has huge rivers and lakes. The Yangtze is the longest river. The Caspian Sea (partly in Europe) is the world's largest saltwater lake. Lake Baikal is the world's deepest lake.

CLIMATE

Northern Asia has long, icy winters and short, cool summers. Most of southern Asia is warm year-round with heavy summer rains.

PLANTS

Areas of coniferous forest called taiga stretch across the north. The central grasslands are known as the Steppes. Rain forests grow in the southeast.

ANIMALS

Tigers, giant pandas, and cobras live in the wild only in Asia.

Two boys direct a camel taxi in the state of Uttar Pradesh. Although they are **desert** animals, camels are used for transportation in many parts of India.

A climber stands at the top of a peak in the **Himalaya.** Mount Everest rises in front of him.

The Three Gorges Dam helps control flooding along the **Yangtze River,** in China.

Mediterranean Sea

Black Sea

CAUCASUS MTS.

Caspian Sea

Dead Sea
Lowest elevation in Asia

Persian Gulf

ARABIAN PENINSULA

Arabian Sea

A F R I C A

0   600 miles
0   900 kilometers

ARCTIC OCEAN

Bering Sea

EUROPE

URAL MOUNTAINS

EUROPE-ASIA BOUNDARY

Ob River

Yenisey River

Irtysh River

Lena River

Amur River

Lake Baikal

THE STEPPES

Aral Sea

TIAN SHAN

GOBI

Yellow River

Indus River

H I M A L A Y A

Brahmaputra

Yangtze River

Ganges River

Mt. Everest
Highest elevation in Asia

Mekong River

PACIFIC OCEAN

South China Sea

Bay of Bengal

INDIAN OCEAN

Sumatra

Borneo

New Guinea

EQUATOR

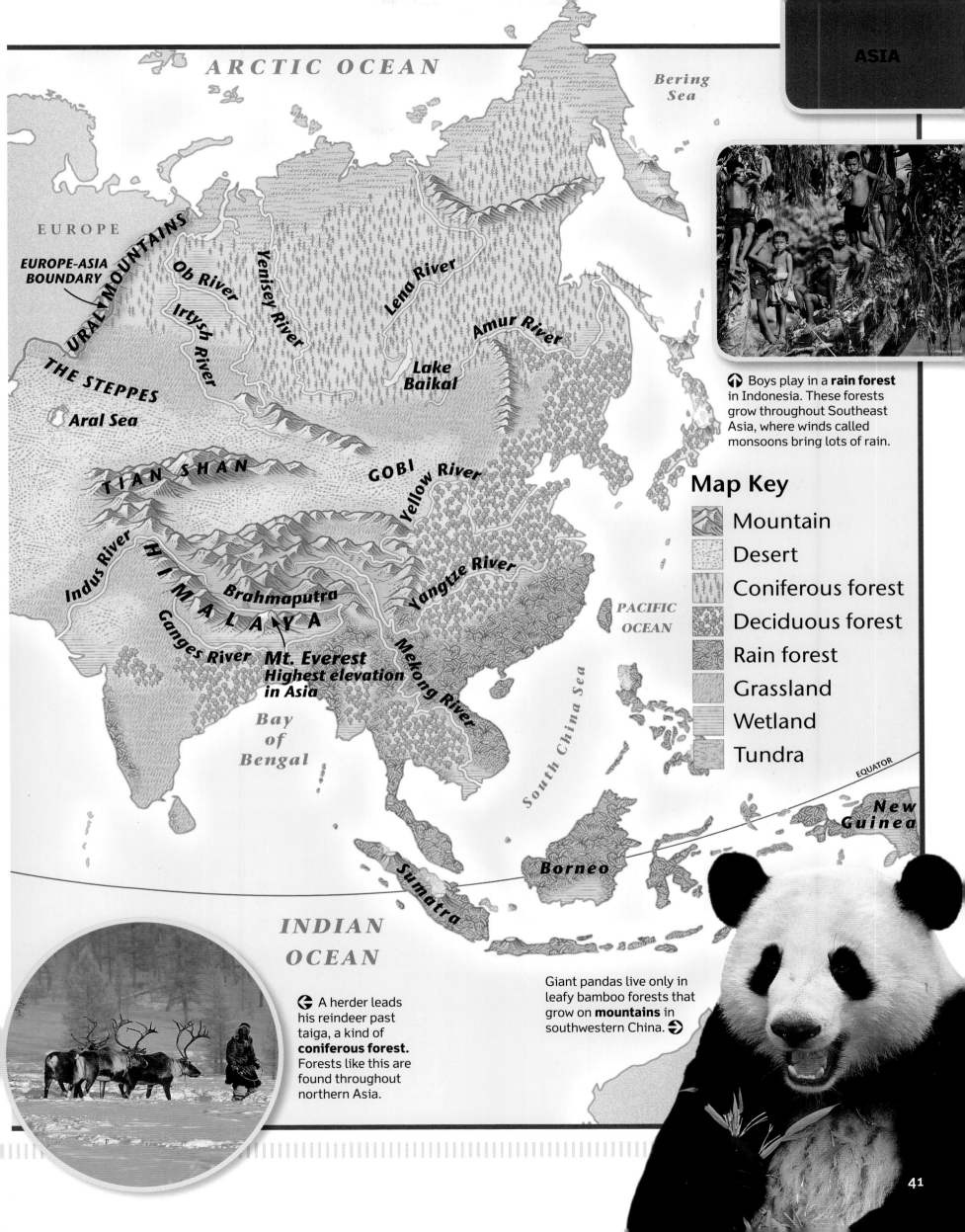

↻ Boys play in a **rain forest** in Indonesia. These forests grow throughout Southeast Asia, where winds called monsoons bring lots of rain.

Map Key

- Mountain
- Desert
- Coniferous forest
- Deciduous forest
- Rain forest
- Grassland
- Wetland
- Tundra

↻ A herder leads his reindeer past taiga, a kind of **coniferous forest.** Forests like this are found throughout northern Asia.

Giant pandas live only in leafy bamboo forests that grow on **mountains** in southwestern China. ➜

41

ASIA

COUNTRIES Asia has 46 countries. China is the largest country with boundaries entirely in Asia. Russia takes up the most area, but it is counted as part of Europe (see pages 36–37). Indonesia is Asia's largest island country.

CITIES Much of Asia is too high, too dry, or too cold for people to live in. Most cities are near the coast or along busy rivers. Tokyo, in Japan, is the largest city.

PEOPLE Asia has more people than any other continent. Each ethnic group has its own language, customs, and appearance. Most people work as farmers or fishermen.

LANGUAGES So many languages are spoken in Asia that even neighbors can have trouble understanding each other. India, for example, has 16 official languages!

PRODUCTS Asia's chief products include rice, wheat, petroleum, cotton, rubber, tea, motor vehicles, and computers.

NOTE: The countries of Russia, Kazakhstan, Azerbaijan, Georgia, and Turkey are in both the continents of Europe and Asia.

These are the Petronas Towers in **Kuala Lumpur,** Malaysia. They are the tallest twin buildings in the world.

This young boy works in a spice market. In **India** people mix lots of spices together to make a strong flavor called curry.

This masked dancer is from **Bali.** Bali is one of more than 3,000 islands that make up the country of Indonesia.

This boy in **Shanghai** draws symbols used in writing the Chinese language. Each symbol stands for a word or an idea.

Map labels:

Baltic Sea
RUSSIA
EUROPE
Moscow
Mediterranean Sea
Black Sea
Istanbul
Ankara
TURKEY
GEORGIA
Tbilisi
ARMENIA
Yerevan
LEBANON
Beirut
SYRIA
AZERBAIJAN
Baku
Caspian Sea
Jerusalem
Damascus
ISRAEL
Amman
JORDAN
Baghdad
Tehran
IRAQ
IRAN
KUWAIT
Kuwait
SAUDI
Riyadh
BAHRAIN
Persian Gulf
QATAR
Doha
Abu Dhabi
ARABIA
UNITED ARAB EMIRATES
Muscat
Sanaa
YEMEN
OMAN
AFRICA
Arabian Sea

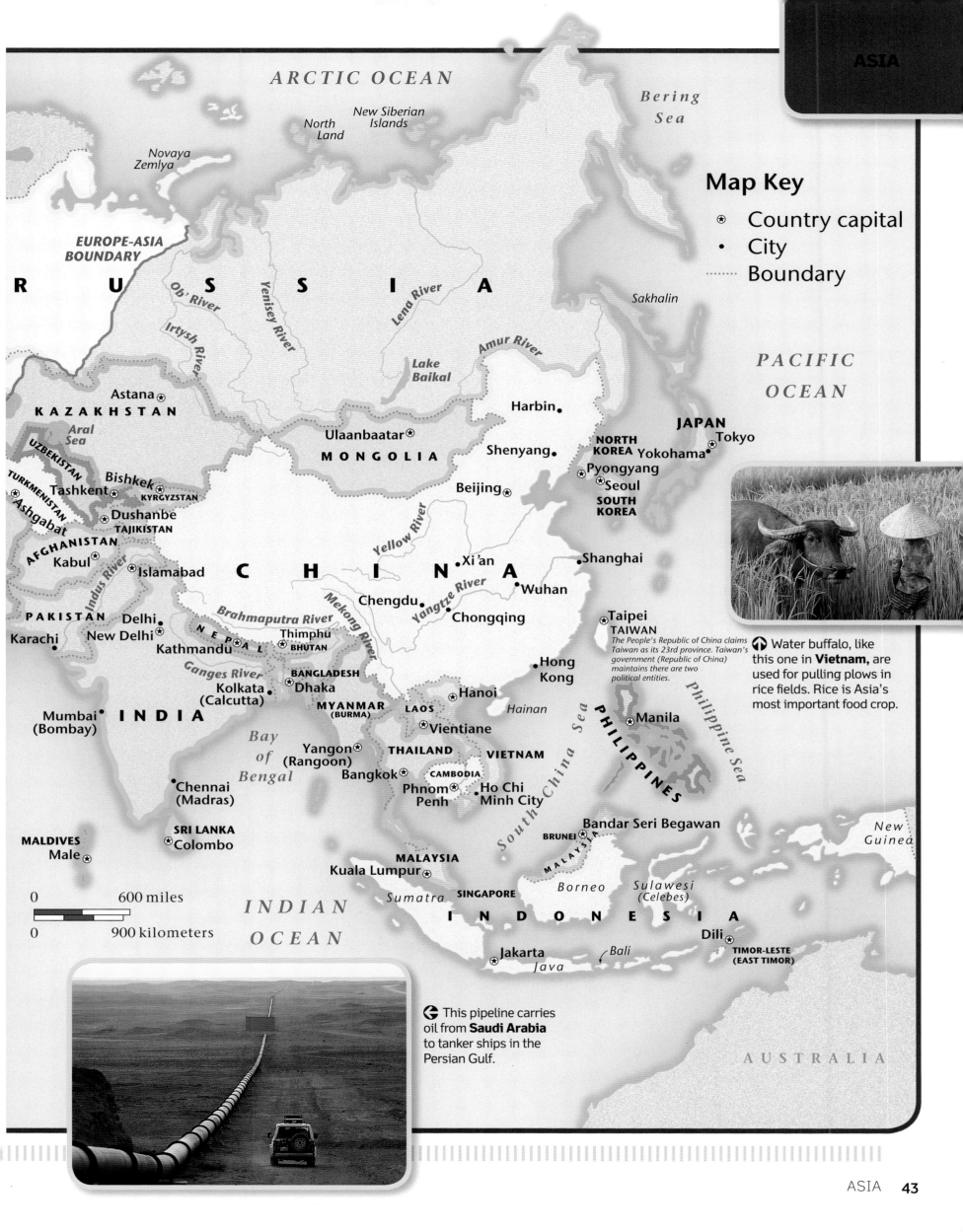

ARCTIC OCEAN

Bering Sea

New Siberian Islands

North Land

Novaya Zemlya

Map Key

⊛ Country capital
• City
.... Boundary

Sakhalin

R U S S I A

EUROPE-ASIA BOUNDARY

Ob' River

Yenisey River

Irtysh River

Lena River

Amur River

Lake Baikal

PACIFIC OCEAN

K A Z A K H S T A N

Astana ⊛

Harbin •

Aral Sea

Ulaanbaatar ⊛

JAPAN

Tokyo

UZBEKISTAN

M O N G O L I A

Shenyang •

NORTH KOREA Yokohama •

TURKMENISTAN

Bishkek ⊛

Tashkent ⊛

Beijing ⊛

⊛ Pyongyang

⊛ Seoul

KYRGYZSTAN

SOUTH KOREA

Ashgabat ⊛

Dushanbe ⊛

TAJIKISTAN

Yellow River

AFGHANISTAN

Kabul ⊛

C H I N A

Xi'an •

Shanghai •

Islamabad ⊛

Chengdu •

Wuhan •

Indus River

Yangtze River

Chongqing •

Taipei •

P A K I S T A N

Delhi •

Brahmaputra River

TAIWAN

The People's Republic of China claims Taiwan as its 23rd province. Taiwan's government (Republic of China) maintains there are two political entities.

Karachi •

New Delhi ⊛

N E P A L

Thimphu ⊛

Mekong River

Kathmandu ⊛

BHUTAN

Hong Kong •

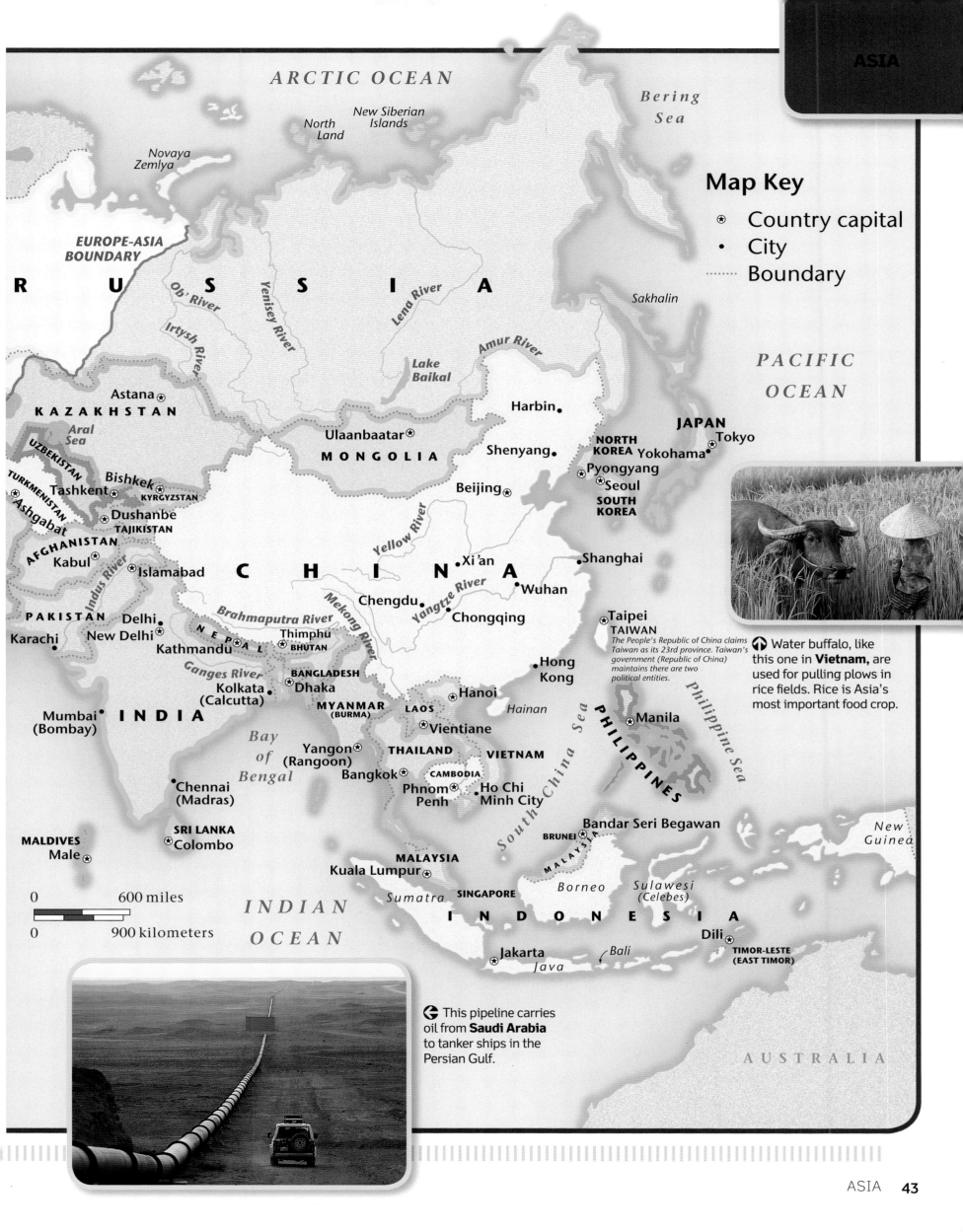
⊕ Water buffalo, like this one in **Vietnam,** are used for pulling plows in rice fields. Rice is Asia's most important food crop.

Ganges River

BANGLADESH

Hanoi •

Kolkata (Calcutta) •

Dhaka ⊛

Hainan

Mumbai (Bombay) •

I N D I A

MYANMAR (BURMA)

LAOS •

Philippine Sea

Bay of Bengal

Vientiane ⊛

Manila •

PHILIPPINES

Yangon (Rangoon) ⊛

THAILAND

VIETNAM

South China Sea

Bangkok ⊛

CAMBODIA

Chennai (Madras) •

Phnom Penh ⊛

Ho Chi Minh City •

Bandar Seri Begawan •

MALDIVES

Male ⊛

SRI LANKA

Colombo ⊛

BRUNEI

New Guinea

Kuala Lumpur ⊛

MALAYSIA

MALAYSIA

Borneo

Sulawesi (Celebes)

0 ——— 600 miles

SINGAPORE

Sumatra

I N D O N E S I A

0 ——— 900 kilometers

I N D I A N O C E A N

Dili ⊛

TIMOR-LESTE (EAST TIMOR)

Jakarta ⊛

Java

Bali

⊖ This pipeline carries oil from **Saudi Arabia** to tanker ships in the Persian Gulf.

A U S T R A L I A

AFRICA

Elephants lumber across the grasslands. Gorillas groom each other in a mountain forest. Hippopotamuses swim in a river. Amazing animals are just part of what Africa has to offer. You can also visit a busy, modern city such as Nairobi, in Kenya; see how diamonds are mined in South Africa; shop in colorful, outdoor markets; take a sailboat ride past temples on the Nile; and climb some of the world's highest sand dunes in Earth's biggest hot desert—the Sahara.

Jambo! Beautiful beadwork is part of a Maasai girl's traditional dress. I live in Kenya where elephants like these roam free. In the distance stands Kilimanjaro, the highest peak in Africa. You can find it on the map on the next page.

AFRICA

Chimpanzees live in Africa's **rain forests.** As many as 50 chimps may live in a group.

 LAND REGIONS Most of Africa is a high, flat plateau. There are few mountains. The Sahara and the Kalahari are among its largest deserts. Rain forests grow along the Equator. Grasslands cover most of the rest of the continent.

 WATER The Nile and the Congo are Africa's longest rivers. Most of Africa's largest lakes are in the Great Rift Valley.

 CLIMATE The Equator crosses Africa's middle, so many places on the continent are hot. It is always wet in the rain forest. Much of the rest of Africa has wet and dry seasons.

 PLANTS Thorny trees called acacias provide food and shade for grassland animals. Date palms grow around desert water holes. Mahogany is one of many kinds of rain forest trees.

 ANIMALS Some of Africa's most familiar animals are shown here. There are also lions and many kinds of antelopes. Lemurs live on Madagascar, Africa's largest island.

Giraffes are the world's tallest animal. They can tower above trees that grow on **grasslands.**

Giant sand dunes in the **Sahara** tower high above this jeep. This huge desert covers most of northern Africa.

Victoria Falls, on the Zambezi River, is one of Africa's wonders. Its African name means "smoke that thunders."

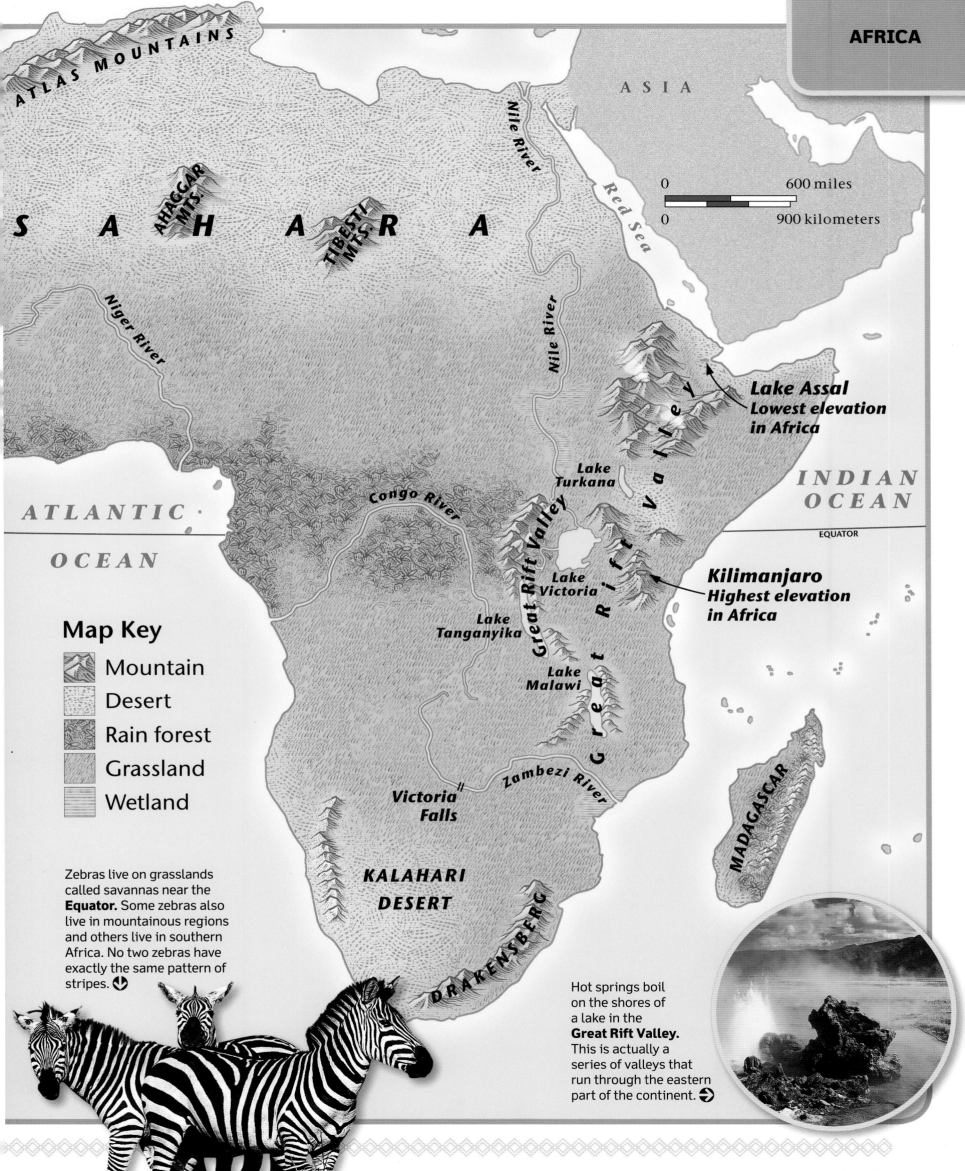

ATLAS MOUNTAINS

ASIA

S A H A R A

AHAGGAR MTS.

TIBESTI MTS.

Nile River

Red Sea

0 ___ 600 miles

0 ___ 900 kilometers

Niger River

Nile River

Lake Assal
Lowest elevation in Africa

Congo River

ATLANTIC

Lake Turkana

INDIAN OCEAN

OCEAN

Great Rift Valley

Lake Victoria

Great Rift Valley

EQUATOR

Kilimanjaro
Highest elevation in Africa

Map Key

- Mountain
- Desert
- Rain forest
- Grassland
- Wetland

Lake Tanganyika

Lake Malawi

Zambezi River

MADAGASCAR

Victoria Falls

Zebras live on grasslands called savannas near the **Equator.** Some zebras also live in mountainous regions and others live in southern Africa. No two zebras have exactly the same pattern of stripes.

KALAHARI DESERT

DRAKENSBERG

Hot springs boil on the shores of a lake in the **Great Rift Valley.** This is actually a series of valleys that run through the eastern part of the continent.

AFRICA

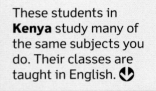

These boys are picking dates. **Algeria** is a leading producer of this fruit.

COUNTRIES Most of Africa's 54 countries were ruled by European countries from the late 1800s to the 1960s. Sudan has the most land. Nigeria has the most people.

CITIES Cairo and Lagos are Africa's biggest cities. Both are on large rivers near the coast. More people live in villages and on farms than in cities.

PEOPLE People in northern Africa's largest countries are mostly Arabs. Most black Africans live south of the Sahara in hundreds of different ethnic groups. Most Europeans live in South Africa.

LANGUAGES Arabic is spoken in the north. Native languages are spoken south of the Sahara. English, French, and Portuguese are the main European languages.

PRODUCTS Africa is a leading producer of cocoa beans, gold, diamonds, and petroleum.

These students in **Kenya** study many of the same subjects you do. Their classes are taught in English.

Canary Islands (Spain)

MOR

WESTERN SAHARA (Morocco)

MAURITANIA

Nouakchott

CAPE VERDE

Praia

Dakar

SENEGAL

Banjul

GAMBIA

Bissau

GUINEA-BISSAU

M

Bamako

GUINEA

Conakry

Freetown

SIERRA LEONE

LIBERIA

Monrovia

CÔTE D'IVOIRE (IVORY COAST)

Small sailboats called feluccas carry goods to trade along the **Nile.** This river is the longest in Africa.

The Sphinx and the pyramid behind it were built by people who lived in **Egypt** thousands of years ago.

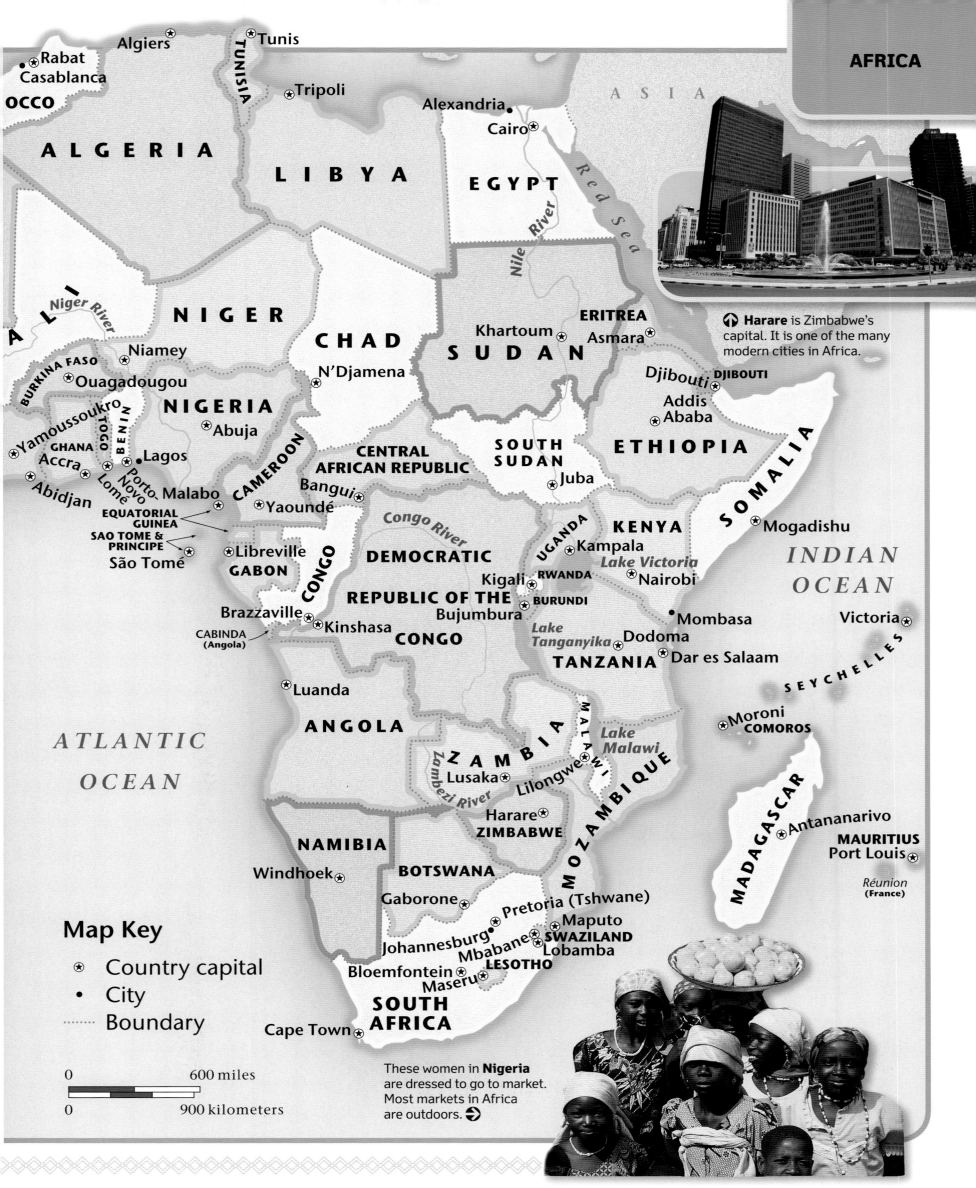

AFRICA

Rabat
Casablanca
OCCO
Algiers ⊛ Tunis ⊛ **TUNISIA**
⊛ Tripoli

ALGERIA

LIBYA

Alexandria •
Cairo ⊛

EGYPT

A S I A

Red Sea

Nile River

L I ·
A

Niger River

N I G E R

⊛ Niamey

BURKINA FASO
⊛ Ouagadougou

NIGERIA

⊛ Abuja

Yamoussoukro
GHANA
Accra ⊛
TOGO
BENIN
Lomé Porto Novo
Abidjan ⊛ • Lagos
Malabo

EQUATORIAL GUINEA →
SAO TOME & PRINCIPE →
São Tomé ⊛

C H A D

N'Djamena ⊛

CAMEROON
Bangui •
⊛ Yaoundé

Libreville ⊛
GABON
CONGO

DEMOCRATIC

REPUBLIC OF THE
Brazzaville ⊛
CONGO
CABINDA (Angola) →
⊛ Kinshasa

Khartoum ⊛
S U D A N

ERITREA
Asmara ⊛

Djibouti ⊛ **DJIBOUTI**

Addis Ababa ⊛

SOUTH SUDAN
⊛ Juba

ETHIOPIA

S O M A L I A

Congo River

UGANDA
Kampala ⊛
KENYA
Lake Victoria
Kigali ⊛ **RWANDA**
Nairobi ⊛
Bujumbura ⊛ **BURUNDI**
Lake Tanganyika
Dodoma ⊛
• Mombasa
⊛ Mogadishu

⊛ Harare is Zimbabwe's capital. It is one of the many modern cities in Africa.

I N D I A N
O C E A N

Victoria ⊛

⊛ Luanda

A T L A N T I C

O C E A N

ANGOLA

Zambezi River
Z A M B I A
Lusaka ⊛

MALAWI
Lilongwe ⊛
Lake Malawi

TANZANIA Dar es Salaam

S E Y C H E L L E S

Moroni ⊛
COMOROS

MADAGASCAR
Antananarivo ⊛

NAMIBIA

Windhoek ⊛

BOTSWANA

Gaborone ⊛

Harare ⊛
ZIMBABWE

M O Z A M B I Q U E

Pretoria (Tshwane) ⊛
Maputo ⊛
Johannesburg •
Mbabane ⊛ **SWAZILAND**
Lobamba

MAURITIUS
Port Louis ⊛

Réunion (France)

Map Key

⊛ Country capital
• City
.... Boundary

Bloemfontein ⊛
Maseru ⊛ **LESOTHO**

SOUTH AFRICA

Cape Town ⊛

0 _____ 600 miles
0 _____ 900 kilometers

These women in **Nigeria** are dressed to go to market. Most markets in Africa are outdoors. ➔

AUSTRALIA

Australia is a most unusual place. It is Earth's smallest and flattest continent and one of the driest, too. It has many large deserts. "Aussies," as Australians like to call themselves, nicknamed their continent the "land down under." That's because the entire continent lies south of, or "under," the Equator. Most Australians live in cities along the coast. But Australia also has huge cattle and sheep ranches. Many ranch children live far from school. They get their lessons by mail or from the Internet or the radio. Their doctors even visit by airplane!

Awa! I'm an Aborigine, one of Australia's native people. My face is painted for a special ceremony in the outback. Behind me is the Great Barrier Reef. It is the world's largest coral reef system, and home to many sea creatures.

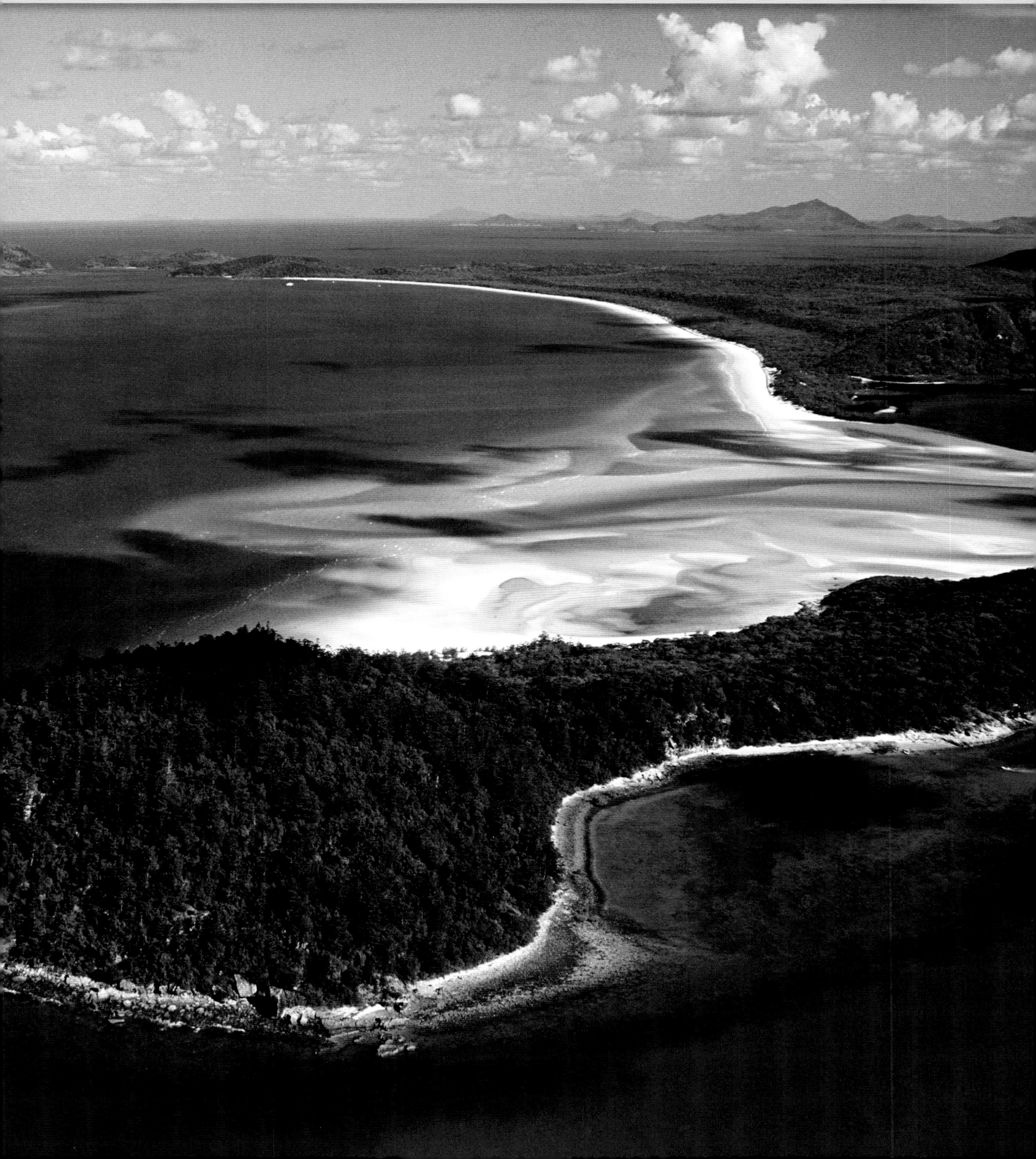

AUSTRALIA

LAND REGIONS The Great Dividing Range stretches along the east coast and into Tasmania. Most of the rest of Australia is a plateau covered by grasslands and deserts.

WATER The Darling, Australia's longest river, is dry during part of the year. So is Lake Eyre, the continent's largest lake. Water lies underground in the Great Artesian Basin.

CLIMATE Most of the continent is very dry. Winds called monsoons bring heavy seasonal rains to the northern coast. Southern Australia can be cold in winter, but much of the continent is warm year-round.

PLANTS Eucalyptuses, or gum trees, and acacias are the most common kinds of plants. They grow throughout Australia.

ANIMALS Australia has many unusual mammals. Koalas and kangaroos raise their young in pouches on their bellies. The platypus is a mammal that has a bill like a duck's. Its babies hatch from eggs.

⮕ The "Three Sisters" rock formation is a stunning site in the Blue Mountains of Australia. These mountains are part of the **Great Dividing Range.**

⮕ A kangaroo warning sign sits along a road leading to Ayers Rock, an ancient rock formation located in Australia's **Western Plateau.** To the Aborigines it is known as Uluru.

⮕ Limestone towers rise above a **desert** in Western Australia. Desert covers much of the continent.

⮕ Koalas live only in **eucalyptus forests.** At one time koalas almost became extinct. Now they are protected by strict laws.

⮕ The cackling laugh of the kookaburra is a familiar **forest** sound.

I N D

O C E

Hamersley Range

Darling Range

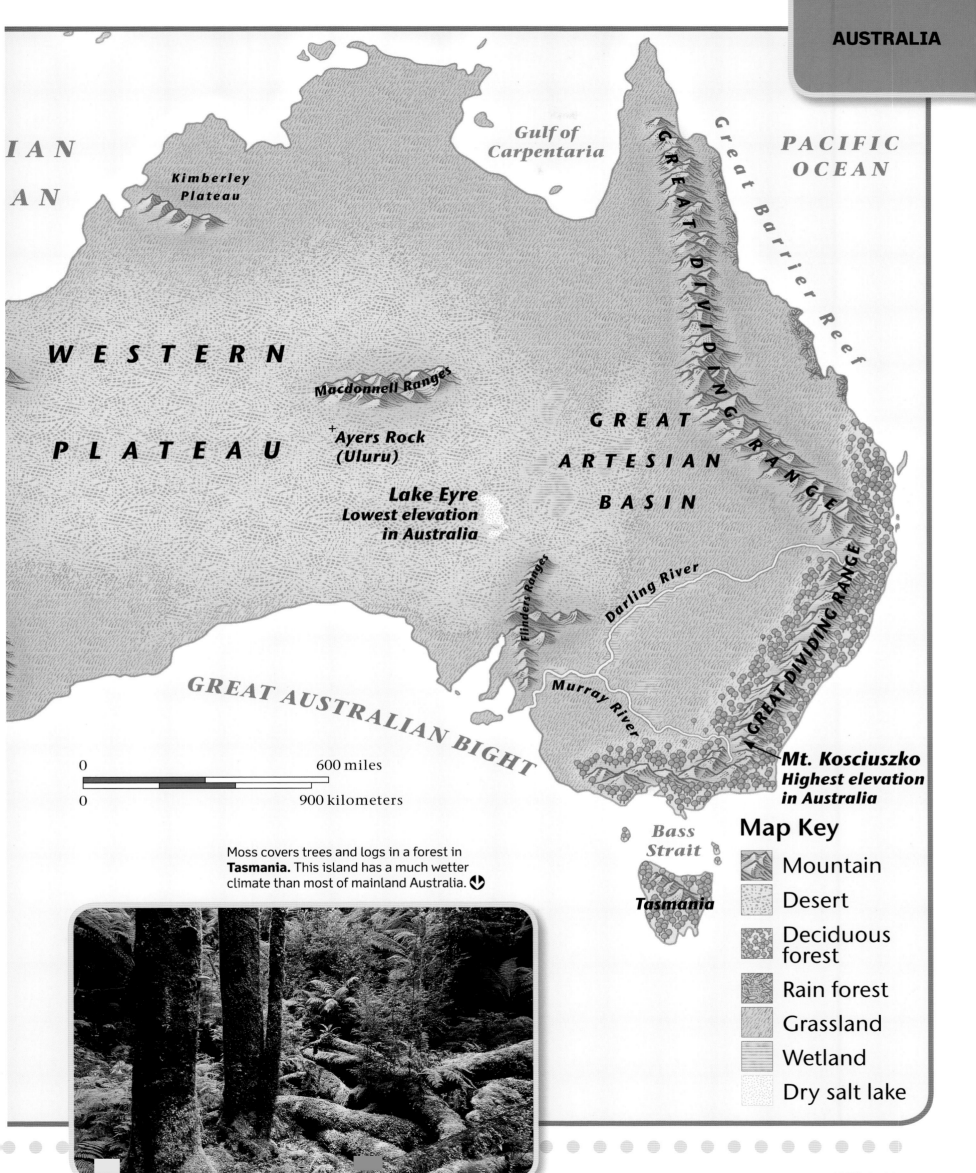

PACIFIC OCEAN

Gulf of Carpentaria

Kimberley Plateau

Great Barrier Reef

GREAT DIVIDING RANGE

W E S T E R N

P L A T E A U

Macdonnell Ranges

+Ayers Rock (Uluru)

G R E A T

A R T E S I A N

B A S I N

Lake Eyre
Lowest elevation in Australia

Flinders Ranges

Darling River

GREAT DIVIDING RANGE

Murray River

GREAT AUSTRALIAN BIGHT

| 0 | | 600 miles |
| 0 | | 900 kilometers |

Mt. Kosciuszko
Highest elevation in Australia

Bass Strait

Tasmania

Moss covers trees and logs in a forest in **Tasmania.** This island has a much wetter climate than most of mainland Australia.

Map Key

⛰ Mountain

Desert

Deciduous forest

Rain forest

Grassland

Wetland

Dry salt lake

AUSTRALIA

COUNTRIES Australia is the only continent that is also a country. It is divided into six states—including Tasmania—and two territories.

CITIES All the chief cities are near the coast—even the capital, Canberra. Sydney has the most people, followed by Melbourne, Brisbane, and Perth.

PEOPLE Most Australians are descendants of settlers from the United Kingdom and Ireland. Aborigines came to Australia from Asia some 40,000 years ago.

LANGUAGES English is the main language of Australia. Aborigines speak some 250 different languages.

PRODUCTS Australia's chief products include wool, beef, wheat, fruits, bauxite, coal, uranium, and diamonds. Most manufactured goods are imported.

⊕ This Aborigine is playing a wooden pipe called a didgeridoo. Many of Australia's native people live in the **Northern Territory.**

⊕ The world's largest cultured pearls are grown in oyster beds along Australia's **northern coast.**

⊕ Surfing is a popular sport in Australia. There is a city near **Brisbane** named Surfers Paradise.

Port Hedland •

⊕ A monorail zips people around **Sydney.** The city is a busy port and the capital of the state of New South Wales.

⊙ **Perth**

⊕ Cafés, like this one, can be hundreds of miles apart in the **outback.** Few people live in this dry, central region.

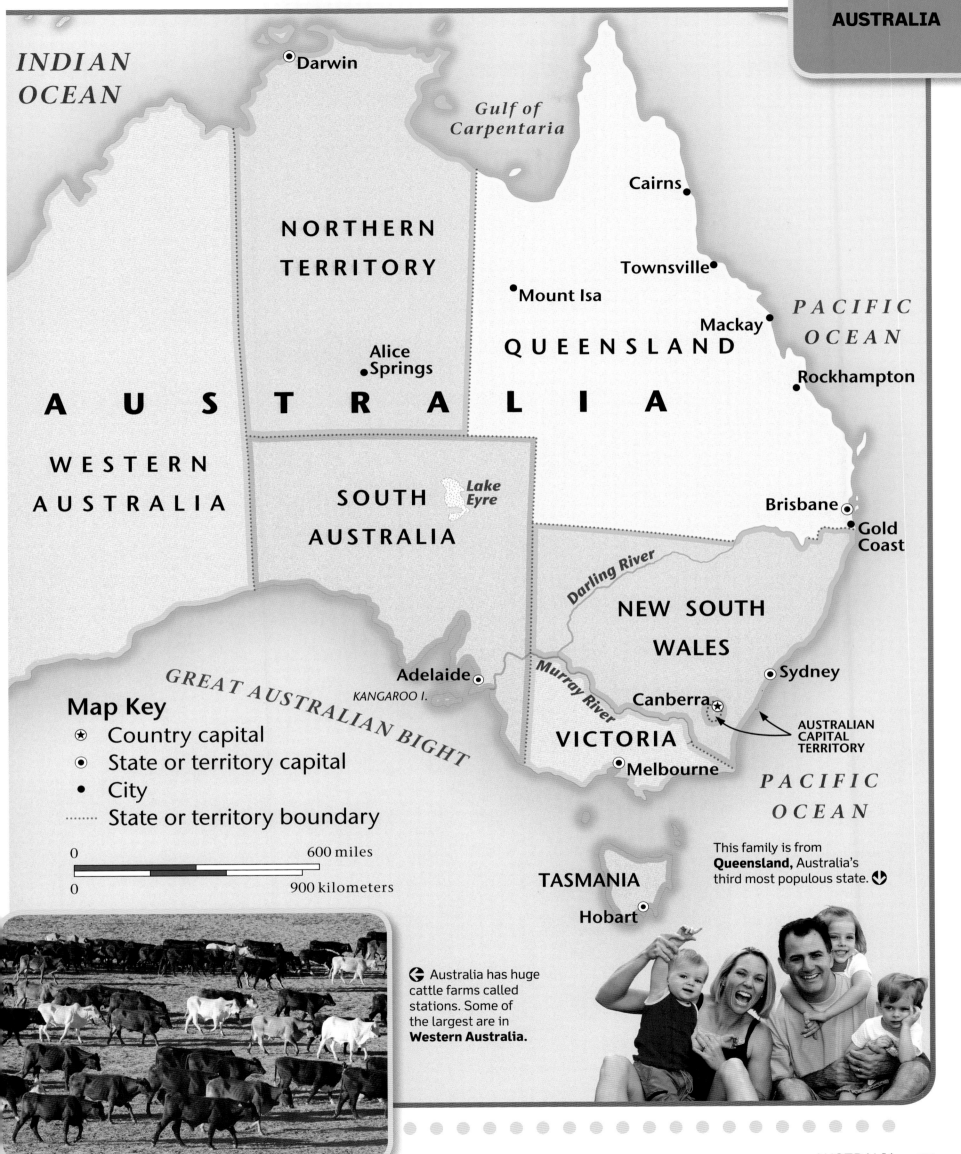

INDIAN OCEAN

•Darwin

Gulf of Carpentaria

NORTHERN TERRITORY

Cairns•

Townsville•

•Mount Isa

QUEENSLAND

PACIFIC OCEAN

Alice •Springs

A U S T R A L I A

Mackay•

•Rockhampton

WESTERN AUSTRALIA

SOUTH AUSTRALIA

Lake Eyre

Brisbane◉
•Gold Coast

Darling River

NEW SOUTH WALES

◉Sydney

Murray River

Canberra◉⊛

AUSTRALIAN CAPITAL TERRITORY

Adelaide◉

KANGAROO I.

Map Key
- ⊛ Country capital
- ◉ State or territory capital
- • City
- ⋯⋯ State or territory boundary

GREAT AUSTRALIAN BIGHT

VICTORIA

◉Melbourne

PACIFIC OCEAN

0		600 miles

0		900 kilometers

This family is from **Queensland**, Australia's third most populous state. ⬇

TASMANIA

Hobart◉

↩ Australia has huge cattle farms called stations. Some of the largest are in **Western Australia**.

ANTARCTICA

Brrrr! Antarctica takes first place as the coldest continent. It is the land around the South Pole. An ice cap two miles thick in places covers most of the land. Temperatures rarely get above freezing. It is also the only continent that has no countries. It has research stations but no cities. The only people are scientists, explorers, and tourists. Everyone stays for awhile, then goes home. The largest land animals that live here year-round are a few kinds of insects!

Chances are you'll see more penguins than people if you visit Antarctica. Like the whale behind them, these penguins depend on the ocean for food. They come ashore to have their babies.

ANTARCTICA

ATLANTIC OCEAN

SOUTH AMERICA

PACIFIC OCEAN

ANTARCTIC

ELLSWORTH

Bellingshausen Sea

Amundsen Sea

LAND REGIONS The Trans-antarctic Mountains divide the continent into two parts. East Antarctica, where the South Pole is located, is mostly a high, flat, icy area. West Antarctica is mountainous. Vinson Massif is the highest peak.

WATER Most of Earth's fresh water is frozen in Antarctica's ice cap. The ice breaks off when it meets the sea. These huge floating chunks of ice in the ocean are called icebergs.

CLIMATE Antarctica is windy and dry. It gets very little snow. Most of the snow that falls turns to ice. The thick ice cap has built up over millions of years.

PLANTS Billions of tiny plants live in the surrounding oceans. Mosses and lichens grow on the land.

ANIMALS Penguins and other seabirds nest on the coast. Whales, seals, and tiny shrimplike animals called krill live in the oceans.

The **Dry Valleys** are bare, rocky places with ice-covered lakes. The tents belong to scientists who say this region looks like Mars.

Few people have ever climbed Antarctica's mountains. This one is called "the Razor." It is near the coast in **Queen Maud Land.**

Elephant seals come ashore along the rocky **Antarctic Peninsula** during the summer.

Jellyfish grow very large under the **sea ice** around the continent. Here they have few enemies so they live a long time.

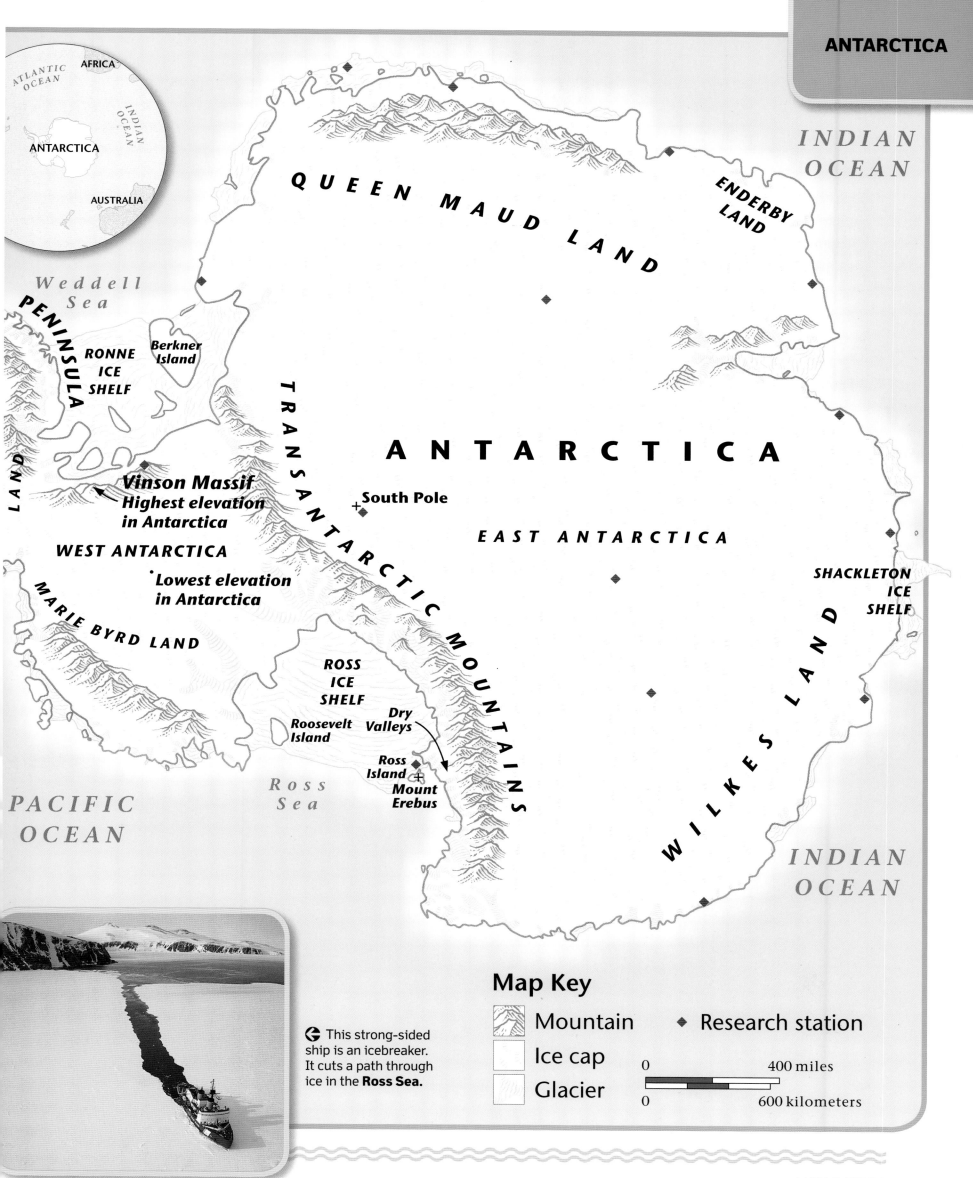

AFRICA

ATLANTIC
OCEAN

INDIAN
OCEAN

ANTARCTICA

AUSTRALIA

INDIAN
OCEAN

ENDERBY
LAND

QUEEN MAUD LAND

*Weddell
Sea*

PENINSULA

RONNE
ICE
SHELF

*Berkner
Island*

LAND

TRANSANTARCTIC MOUNTAINS

ANTARCTICA

Vinson Massif
Highest elevation
in Antarctica

South Pole

WEST ANTARCTICA

EAST ANTARCTICA

•**Lowest elevation**
in Antarctica

MARIE BYRD LAND

SHACKLETON
ICE
SHELF

ROSS
ICE
SHELF

Roosevelt
Island

Dry
Valleys

WILKES LAND

Ross
Island
Mount
Erebus

*Ross
Sea*

**PACIFIC
OCEAN**

INDIAN
OCEAN

Map Key

Mountain   ◆ Research station

Ice cap

Glacier

⟳ This strong-sided
ship is an icebreaker.
It cuts a path through
ice in the **Ross Sea.**

| 0 | 400 miles |
| 0 | 600 kilometers |

WORLD AT A GLANCE

LAND
The Continents, Largest to Smallest

1. **Asia:** 17,208,000 sq mi (44,570,000 sq km)
2. **Africa:** 11,608,000 sq mi (60,065,000 sq km)
3. **North America:** 9,449,000 sq mi (24,474,000 sq km)
4. **South America:** 6,880,000 sq mi (17,819,000 sq km)
5. **Antarctica:** 5,100,000 sq mi (13,209,000 sq km)
6. **Europe:** 3,841,000 sq mi (9,947,000 sq km)
7. **Australia:** 2,970,000 sq mi (7,692,000 sq km)

WATER
The Oceans, Largest to Smallest

1. **Pacific Ocean:** 65,436,200 sq mi (169,479,000 sq km)
2. **Atlantic Ocean:** 35,338,500 sq mi (91,526,400 sq km)
3. **Indian Ocean:** 28,839,800 sq mi (74,694,700 sq km)
4. **Arctic Ocean:** 5,390,000 sq mi (13,960,100 sq km)

Highest, Longest, Largest
The numbers below show locations on the map.

1 **Highest Mountain on a Continent**
Mt. Everest, in Asia: 29,035 ft (8,850 m)

2 **Largest Island**
Greenland, borders the Arctic and Atlantic Oceans:
836,000 sq mi (2,166,000 sq km)

3 **Largest Ocean**
Pacific Ocean: 65,436,200 sq mi
(169,479,000 sq km)

4 **Longest River**
Nile River, in Africa:
4,400 mi (7,081 km)

5 **Largest Freshwater Lake**
Lake Superior, in North America:
31,700 sq mi (82,100 sq km)

6 **Largest Saltwater Lake**
Caspian Sea, in Europe-Asia:
143,000 sq mi (371,000 sq km)

7 **Largest Hot Desert**
Sahara, in Africa: 3,475,000 sq mi
(9,000,000 sq km)

8 **Largest Cold Desert**
Antarctica: 5,100,000 sq mi (13,209,000 sq km)

PEOPLE

Almost seven billion people live on Earth—enough to fill a string of school buses that would circle the Equator almost 24 times! More than half the world's people live in Asia.

Five Largest Countries by Number of People

1. **China, Asia:** 1,336,718,000 people
2. **India, Asia:** 1,189,173,000 people
3. **United States, North America:** 313,232,000 people
4. **Indonesia, Asia:** 245,613,000 people
5. **Brazil, South America:** 203,430,000 people

Five Largest Cities* by Number of People

1. **Tokyo, Japan (Asia):** 36,670,000 people
2. **Delhi, India (Asia):** 22,160,000 people
3. **São Paulo, Brazil (South America):** 20,260,000 people
4. **Mumbai (Bombay), India (Asia):** 20,040,000 people
5. **Mexico City, Mexico (North America):** 19,460,000 people

*Figures are for metropolitan areas.

GLOSSARY

bauxite a substance mined from the Earth that is the chief source of aluminum

capital city a place where a country's government is located

city a settled place where people work in jobs other than farming

coral reef a stony formation in warm, shallow ocean water that is made up of the skeletons of tiny sea animals called corals

country a place that has boundaries, a name, a flag, and a government that is the highest worldly authority over the land and the people who live there

environment the world around you, including people, cities, beliefs, plants and animals, air, water—everything

ethnic group people who share a common ancestry, language, beliefs, and traditions

European Union an organization of 27 European countries (Austria,* Belgium,* Bulgaria, Cyprus,* Czech Republic, Denmark, Estonia,* Finland,* France,* Germany,* Greece,* Hungary, Ireland,* Italy,* Latvia, Lithuania, Luxembourg,* Malta,* Netherlands,* Poland, Portugal,* Romania, Slovakia,* Slovenia,* Spain,* Sweden, and United Kingdom)

glacier a large, slow-moving mass of ice; glaciers that cover huge areas are called ice caps

lemur an animal related to monkeys that is active at night and lives mostly in forests on Madagascar, in Africa

lichen a plantlike organism that is part alga and part fungus and that usually lives where few plants can survive

*The euro is the country's official currency.

mosses nonflowering, low-growing green plants that grow on rocks and trees throughout the world

outback the name Australians use for the dry interior region of their country where few people live

plains large areas of mainly flat land often covered with grasses

province a unit of government similar to a state

state a unit of government that takes up a specific area within a country, as in one of the 50 large political units in the United States

Steppes a Russian name for the grasslands that stretch from eastern Europe into Asia

taiga a Russian word for the scattered, coniferous forests that grow in cold, northern regions

Pronunciations

Note: Syllables printed in all capital letters should be accented.

Aborigine ah buh RIJ uh nee

Ayers ARZ

Baikal by KALL

bauxite BAWK site

Buenos Aires bway nus AR eez

didgeridoo DIH juh ree doo

eucalyptus you kuh LIP tus

Eyre AR

felucca fuh LOO kuh

Harare hah RAH ray

Himalaya him uh LAY uh

Kalahari ka luh HAR ee

Kilimanjaro kih luh mun JAR o

Kinshasa kin SHAH suh

koala kuh WAH luh

Latvia LAT vee uh

lichen LIE kun

Liechtenstein LIKT un stine

Maasai MAH sigh

Monaco MAH nuh ko

Nigeria nigh JIR ee uh

Quechua KEH chuh wuh

Rio de Janeiro REE oo dee zha NAY roo

San Marino san muh REE no

Sudan soo DAN

Sumatra suh MAH truh

taiga TIE guh

Tasmania taz MAY nee uh

Uluru oo LOO roo

Yangtze yang SEE

Zambezi zam BEE zee

Zimbabwe zim BAH bway

Greetings in Native Languages

awa AH wuh
an Australian Aborigine word for a friendly "hello"

imaynalla ee my NAH yuh
"greetings" in Quechua, a Native American language of South America

jambo JAM bo
"hello" in Swahili, a language spoken throughout East Africa

kha-hay kaw HAY
"greetings" in Crow, a Native American language of the United States

namasté no mah STAY
"I salute you" in Hindi, one of the many languages of India, in Asia

sveiks SVAYKS
"hello" in Latvian, the language of Latvia, a country in eastern Europe

INDEX

Pictures and the text that describes them have their page numbers printed in **bold** type.

Published by the National Geographic Society

John M. Fahey, Jr.,
Chairman of the Board and Chief Executive Officer

Timothy T. Kelly, *President*

Declan Moore, *Executive Vice President; President, Publishing*

Melina Gerosa Bellows,
*Executive Vice President, Chief Executive Officer,
Books, Kids and Family*

Prepared by the Book Division

Nancy Laties Feresten,
Senior Vice President, Editor in Chief, Children's Books

Jonathan Halling,
Design Director, Books and Children's Publishing

Jennifer Emmett,
Editorial Director, Children's Books

Carl Mehler, *Director of Maps*

R. Gary Colbert, *Production Director*

Jennifer A. Thornton, *Managing Editor*

Staff for This Book

Priyanka Lamichhane, *Project Editor*
David M. Seager, *Art Director*
Lori Epstein, Senior *Illustrations Editor*
Ruth Thompson, *Designer*
Kate Olesin, *Editorial Assistant*
Kathryn Robbins, *Design Production Assistant*
Hillary Moloney, *Illustrations Assistant*
Stuart Armstrong, John S. Ballay, Thomas L. Gray,
Michael McNey, David B. Miller, Joseph F. Ochlak,
Michelle H. Picard, Nicholas P. Rosenbach, Tibor G. Tóth,
Gregory Ugiansky, Martin S. Walz,
Map Research, Editing, and Production
Martha B. Sharma, *Writer and Consultant*
Stuart Armstrong, *Graphics Illustrator*
Grace Hill, Sam Bardley, *Associate Managing Editors*
Lewis R. Bassford, *Production Manager*
Susan Borke, *Legal and Business Affairs*

Manufacturing and Quality Management

Christopher A. Liedel, *Chief Financial Officer*
Phillip L. Schlosser, *Senior Vice President*
Chris Brown, *Technical Director*
Nicole Elliott, *Manager*
Rachel Faulise, *Manager*
Robert L. Barr, *Manager*

Illustrations Credits

COVER
(climbing girl), Don Mason/Getty Images; (skateboarding boy), Rubberball; (Earth), Ragnarock/Shutterstock; (Statue of Liberty), Digital Stock; (penguin), Jan Martin Will/Shutterstock; (dolphin), Kristian Sekulic/iStockphoto.com; (Roman Colosseum), Maugli/Shutterstock; (snowcapped volcano), LaurensT/Shutterstock

FRONT MATTER
1 (baseball player), David Young-Wolff/PhotoEdit; (Earth), Ragnarock/Shutterstock; (Machu Picchu), Robert Frerck/Getty Images; (giraffe), Michael Busselle/Getty Images; (St. Basil's Cathedral), Jerry Alexander/Getty Images; (panda), Keren Su/Getty Images; 2 (top), Ed Simpson/Getty Images; 2 (bottom), Michael J P Scott/Getty Images; 3 (top, left), Connie Coleman/Getty Images; 3 (top, right), Paul Chesley/Getty Images; 3 (left, center), Gavin Hellier/Robert Harding World Imagery/Corbis; 3 (right, center), Art Wolfe/Getty Images; 3 (bottom), James Martin/Getty Images; 10 (left), John Warden/Getty Images; 10 (center), Hugh Sitton/Getty Images; 10 (right), Steven Sweinberg/Getty Images; 11 (top), Andrea Booher/Getty Images; 11 (top, center), Greg Probst/Getty Images; 11 (bottom, center), Stephen and Michele Vaughan; 11 (bottom, left), Cosmo Condina/Getty Images; 11 (bottom, center), Michael Nichols, NGP; 11 (bottom, right), Tom Bean/Getty Images; 14 (top), John Noble; 14 (top, left), Bruno De Hogues/Getty Images; 14 (bottom, left), Jack Dykinga/Getty Images; 14 (bottom, right), Alison Wright/NationalGeographicStock.com; 15 (left, center), A. Witte/C. Mahaney/Getty Images; 15 (top, left), Stuart McCall/Getty Images; 15 (top, right), Chad Ehlers/Getty Images; 15 (left, center), A. Witte/C. Mahaney/Getty Images; 15 (center), Martine Mouchy; 15 (bottom), Mark Harris/Getty Images

NORTH AMERICA
16, Ed Simpson/Getty Images; 16–17, Yva Momatiuk & John Eastcott/Minden Pictures; 18 (top), Charles Krebs/Getty Images; 18 (top center), Stephen Krasemann/Getty Images; 18 (bottom, center), Mark Lewis/Getty Images; 18 (bottom, left), Bruce Wilson/Getty Images; 18–19, James Randklev/Getty Images; 19, Charles Krebs/Getty Images; 20 (top), Robcocquyt/Shutterstock; 20 (top, center), George Hunter; 20 (bottom, center, left), Mark Lewis/Getty Images; 20 (bottom, center, right), Cosmo Condina/Getty Images; 20 (bottom, left), Nick Gunderson/Getty Images; 20 (bottom, right), Alison Wright/Corbis; 21, Will & Deni McIntyre/Getty Images; 22 (top), Jake Rajs/Getty Images; 22 (center), Billy Hustace/Getty Images; 22 (bottom), David Young-Wolff/PhotoEdit; 23 (top), Pete Seaward/Getty Images; 23 (bottom, left), Philip Coblentz/Corbis; 23 (bottom, right), Jim Richardson; 24 (top), Tim Thompson; 24 (center), Cosmo Condina/Getty Images; 24 (bottom), Mike Casesse/Corbis; 25 (top), Chris Tomaidis/Getty Images; 25 (center), T. Davis & W. Bilenduke/Getty Images; 25 (bottom), Wayne R. Bilenduke/Getty Images

SOUTH AMERICA
26, Michael J P Scott/Getty Images; 26–27, Robert Frerck/Getty Images; 28 (top), Bryan Parsley; 28 (top, center), William J Hebert/Getty Images; 28 (bottom, center), James R. Holland; 28 (bottom, left), Frans Lanting; 28 (bottom, right), Nicholas Divore/Getty Images; 30 (top), Lori Epstein/www.loriepstein.com; 30 (top, center), Gary Yim/Shutterstock; 30 (bottom, center), RJ Lerich/Shutterstock; 30 (bottom, left), Robert Frerk/Getty Images; 30 (bottom, right), Don Kincaid/Stars and Stripes; 31, Ary Diesendruck/Getty Images

EUROPE
32, Connie Coleman/Getty Images; 32–33, BL Images Ltd./Alamy; 34 (top), James Balog/Getty Images; 34 (center), Michael Busselle/Getty Images; 34 (bottom, left), Bruce Coleman Ltd.; 34 (bottom, right), Art Wolfe/Getty Images; 35, Richard Passmore/Getty Images; 36 (top), Vladitto/Shutterstock; 36 (center), Maarten Udema Photography; 36 (bottom, center), Medio Images/Index Stock Imagery; 36 (bottom, center), Fotosearch; 36 (bottom, left), Yann Layma/Getty Images; 36 (bottom, right), unknown 1861/Shutterstock; 37, Anthony Cassidy/Getty Images

ASIA
38, Gavin Hellier/Robert Harding World Imagery/Corbis; 38–39, John W. Banagan/Getty Images; 40 (top), Chris Noble/Getty Images; 40 (center), Robert Morton/iStockphoto.com; 40 (bottom), Alison Wright/NationalGeographicStock.com; 41 (top), James Nelson/Getty Images; 41 (bottom, left), Paul Harris/Getty Images; 41 (bottom, right), Keren Su/Getty Images; 42 (top), Pistolseven/Shutterstock; 42 (center), Nicholas DeVore/Getty Images; 42, (bottom, left), Kenneth Love; 42 (bottom, right), Michael Ventura; 43 (top), Keren Su/Getty Images; 43 (bottom), Wayne Eastep/Getty Images; 43, Keren Su/STONE/Getty Images

AFRICA
44, James Martin/Getty Images; 44–45, Renee Lynn/Getty Images; 46 (top), Tim Davis/Getty Images; 46 (center), Hugh Sitton/Getty Images; 46 (bottom, left), Michael Busselle/Getty Images; 46 (bottom, right), Chad Ehlers/Getty Images; 47 (left), Kevin Shafer/Getty Images; 47 (right), Michael Busselle/Getty Images; 48 (top), Will & Deni McIntyre/Getty Images; 48 (top, center), Paul Kenward/Getty Images; 48 (bottom, center), Hugh Sitton/Getty Images; 48 (bottom), Sylvain Grandadam/Getty Images; 49 (top), Daniel May/Getty Images; 49 (bottom), Sally Mayman/Getty Images

AUSTRALIA
50, Paul Chesley/Getty Images; 50–51, Peter Hendrie/Getty Images; 52 (top), Wouter Tolenaars/Shutterstock; 52 (top, center), Nic Cleave Photography/Alamy; 52 (bottom, center), Fred Bavendam; 52 (bottom, left), Penny Tweedie/Getty Images; 52 (bottom, right), Andrew Chin/Shutterstock; 53, Bernard Grilly/Getty Images; 54 (top), David Doubilet/NationalGeographicStock.com; 54 (top, center), Myfanwy Jane Webb/iStockphoto.com; 54 (bottom, center), LocalPhotos/Matthew Lambert; 54 (bottom, left), Paul Souders/Getty Images; 54 (bottom, right), Oliver Strewe/Getty Images; 55 (right), Pamspix/iStockphoto.com; 55 (left), John Carnemolla/Shutterstock

ANTARCTICA
56, Art Wolfe/Getty Images; 56–57, Tim Davis/Getty Images; 58 (top), Maria Stenzel; 58 (center), Gordon Wiltsie; 58 (bottom, left), David Madison/Getty Images; 58 (bottom, right), Norbert Wu /www.norbertwu.com; 59, Kim Westerskov/STONE/Getty Images

The National Geographic Society is one of the world's largest nonprofit scientific and educational organizations. Founded in 1888 to "increase and diffuse geographic knowledge," the Society works to inspire people to care about the planet. National Geographic reflects the world through its magazines, television programs, films, music and radio, books, DVDs, maps, exhibitions, live events, school publishing programs, interactive media and merchandise. *National Geographic* magazine, the Society's official journal, published in English and 33 local-language editions, is read by more than 38 million people each month. The National Geographic Channel reaches 320 million households in 34 languages in 166 countries. National Geographic Digital Media receives more than 15 million visitors a month. National Geographic has funded more than 9,400 scientific research, conservation and exploration projects and supports an education program promoting geography literacy. For more information, visit nationalgeographic.com.

For more information, please call 1-800-NGS LINE (647-5463) or write to the following address:
National Geographic Society
1145 17th Street N.W.
Washington, D.C. 20036-4688 U.S.A.

Visit us online at www.nationalgeographic.com/books

For librarians and teachers: www.ngchildrensbooks.org

More for kids from National Geographic:
kids.nationalgeographic.com

For information about special discounts for bulk purchases, please contact National Geographic Books Special Sales: ngspecsales@ngs.org

For rights or permissions inquiries, please contact National Geographic Books Subsidiary Rights:
ngbookrights@ngs.org

The Library of Congress has cataloged the 1999 edition as follows:

National Geographic beginner's world atlas / photographs from Tony Stone Images
p. cm.
Includes index.
Summary: Maps, photographs, illustrations, and text present information about the continents of the world.
ISBN 0-7922-7502-0
1. Children's atlases. [1. Atlases. 2. Geography.] I. Title.
II. Title: Beginner's world atlas
G1021 .N39 1999 <G&M>
912—dc21

Copyright © 1999, 2005, 2011 National Geographic Society;
ISBN 978-1-4263-0838-3 (2011 hardcover); 978-1-4263-0839-0 (reinforced library binding)

Printed in Hong Kong

13/THK/3